The River Cottage Booze Handbook

by John Wright

with an introduction by Hugh Fearnley-Whittingstall

www.rivercottage.net

BLOOMSBURY

LONDON · NEW DELHI · NEW YORK · SYDNEY

For Carol and Jackie

First published in Great Britain 2013

Text © 2013 by John Wright
Photography and illustrations © 2013 by John Wright

The moral right of the author has been asserted

Bloomsbury Publishing Plc, 50 Bedford Square, London WC1B 3DP
Bloomsbury Publishing, London, New Delhi, New York and Sydney
www.bloomsbury.com

A CIP catalogue record for this book is available from the British Library

ISBN 978 1 4088 1793 3
10 9 8 7 6 5 4 3 2 1

Project editor: Janet Illsley
Designer: Will Webb
Indexer: Hilary Bird

Printed and bound in Italy by Graphicom

www.bloomsbury.com/rivercottage
www.rivercottage.net

Contents

I have many reasons to be glad that I know John Wright. There is my confidence, developed over many a shared foraging expedition, that the mushrooms I gather will not kill me. There are the friendly debates, escalating only occasionally to incredulous spluttering, about the finer points of wild food preparation (you should see him trying to peel a chestnut – a fish would do it more effectively). There is my respect for the lengths he will go to in order to reach the topmost damsons on a tree or the remotest patch of sea kale. But one of the things I appreciate most in John is his sound and sensible regard for the subtle art of imbibing. It's a pleasure to spend time with a chap who is so fond of a good tipple.

John has been the wild food expert at River Cottage for many years now. His encyclopaedic knowledge and infectious enthusiasm have inspired countless visitors to gather and enjoy wild food for themselves. This is John's fourth River Cottage handbook. The previous three, focusing on mushrooms, the edible seashore and hedgerow foraging, dealt with fairly immediate ways to consume the wild harvest. This one is more about helping your ingredients take a leap toward immortality, to borrow a phrase, by turning them into liquors and libations that will tickle your fancy and warm your cockles (though some may proceed directly to tickling your cockles) weeks, months and indeed years after the ingredients were gathered. Some of his beer recipes, meanwhile, go beyond the wild food remit, and use the classic base ingredients – barley and hops – from which almost all great ales are born.

There is something more than toastworthy – truly admirable in fact – in brewing your own beers and wines. Showing both the commitment required to gather the raw ingredients and procure the right equipment, and then the restraint needed to blend, bottle and wait until the brew comes good, takes a certain kind of patient determination. John has this in abundance. But it is mingled with a much more raw and immediate quality, a passionate drive to gather the best fruits, to produce ever-better drinks and to find new ways of doing so. Beneath his calm and laconic exterior, he is keen as mustard, driven, a home brewer of extraordinary perspicacity. Come between this man and his must bucket at your peril.

It's this almost paradoxical combination of clear focus and gay abandon, the willingness to go that one step further, to try the next thing or sample a new ingredient, that underlies this book. Truly, if you have any leanings at all towards producing your own liqueurs, wines or ales, you could not have a better guide. You have here all the benefits of John's exhaustive research and experimentation, and, not to be sniffed at, his considerable years of determined drinking experience.

Flick through these pages and I am sure you will be intrigued by the gloriously coloured, scented, flavoured, and indeed titled, concoctions John has brewed up. Who would not be impatient to try rose vodka, Aleister Crowley's bitter (bitter about what, one wonders? The fact that John has stolen his recipe presumably) or even The oldest drink in the world – flavoured by amber, of all things?

John has written an extensive chapter on infusions, the very simplest and most immediate of homemade alcoholic drinks, which do not involve brewing or fermentation at all, just the gentle mingling of fruits, flowers or leaves with a ready-made spirit. If you're new to DIY drink production, I'd urge you to start here – these recipes are for the most part amazingly easy and have very impressive results.

Once you're bitten by the booze bug, you can move on into its slightly more complex dimensions. John unravels the arcane-seeming art of wine-making, laying it bare for the simple chemical process it is, while allowing for the mysterious alchemy that occurs when you throw fruit, sugar and yeast together, and the surprises that may inevitably result from the use of variable wild ingredients. I long ago learned the true value and character of such wines. They are not, as some people seem to think, intended to be imitations of great, grape-based vintages. The idea – or at least my idea, and John Wright's too – is to broaden and enhance your drinking experience, to introduce yourself to a range of flavours and bouquets that you will simply never experience if you stick to shop-bought vino.

I quibble with John on only one point of hedgerow wine-making. It's our ongoing wine-lover's tiff. Birch sap wine (see p.141) can be delicious. And I have a bottle in my wine rack that's going to prove it to him in about a year's time (John's been drinking his just a few months old – too young John, too young!).

John's chapter on brewing beer will set you up to produce ales, stouts, lagers and bitters that really will give the best commercially made beers a run for their money. I've tried a pint of his Ordinary bitter (p.211) and I can tell you it was not ordinary at all. I love the democracy of this chapter, the way it places beer-making back firmly in the common realm, at the fingertips – or, more accurately, in the kitchen, garage or garden shed – of anyone who has a yen for it, just as it always used to be in the days when supping ale was more popular than drinking water.

And even if you put all its technically enabling qualities aside for one moment, you can enjoy this book for the sheer quality of the writing. John is never less than a pleasure to read – brilliant, funny and wise (annoyingly often). If you are not quite ready yet to fill your loft with bubbling demi-johns, you can still savour John's humour and enthusiasm. His wit is as dry as a glass of oak moss gin, and his vision just as clear... although sometimes a little less so following a good sampling session.

But really, I doubt you'll get far into this book without feeling the itch to get brewing. You'll soon be persuaded that liqueur-, wine- and beer-making are the most splendid ways to preserve and celebrate various hedgerow harvests – as well as good ingredients that you've actually paid money for. Soon you'll be raising a toast with a glass of your very own, unique vintage. And I'd be delighted to join you in saluting the author who inspired you. Cheers John!

Hugh Fearnley-Whittingstall, East Devon, September 2013

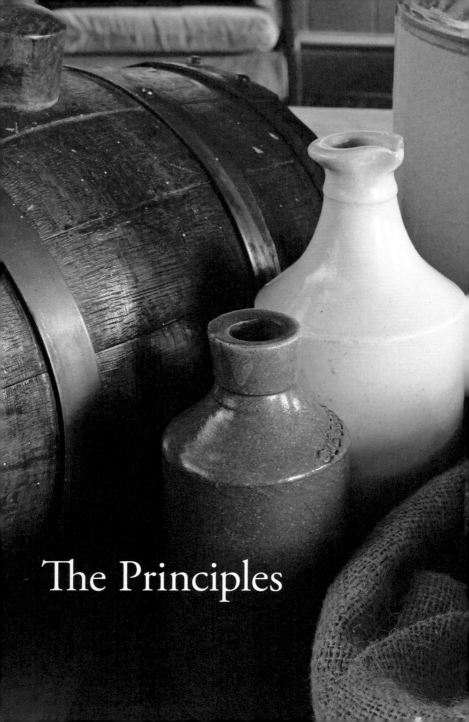

The Principles

I once had a chemistry set but even in the health-and safety-free 1960s it did not include ingredients that could be used to make rockets and bombs (you could get those at the gardening shop). Still, I had fun with test tubes and crucibles and flasks and, on one occasion, slightly poisoning my sister.

Mucking about with glassware and chemicals was a great joy that now finds expression in the only slightly safer processes of home brewing. The dining room, the kitchen, the loft and the shed sport arrays of bottles and potions, tubes and presses, and rows of demi-johns bubbling away melodiously.

I started home brewing over thirty years ago when I moved to West Dorset. I found myself living in a farmhouse where you could gaze for thirty miles over the hills but still not see another house. It was a very old-fashioned farm on which my landlord, Snowy Eyre, a colourful gentleman farmer who would have been more at home in the eighteenth century, bred beef cattle. It was, and mostly still is, an untamed wilderness; more a nature reserve than a farm.

If there was a place designed to encourage the nascent home brewer, this was it. Here I could spend hours picking blackberries, elderberries, dandelion flowers, crab apples, hazelnuts, haws, sloes, rosehips, redcurrants and more. There was so much free food that the temptation to pick was irresistible. But what do you do with 50 kilos of blackberries once you are thoroughly sick of blackberry crumble, what can be made with crab apples other than jelly, and what can you do with sloes and elderberries in the first place?

I bought all the brewing equipment and began. I took the principle of learning by my mistakes very seriously and, it seemed, made as many mistakes as I could. But some of my wines and infusions (I had yet to enter the worlds of beer and cider) turned out very well indeed. Some did not, even though I tried to fool myself into thinking they had. This is a common and lamentable trait among home brewers; they think everything that comes out of their demi-johns and fermenters is ambrosia and worthy of first prize at any county show. Worse, as I know from long and bitter experience, they insist that people try their noxious brews and are affronted if anyone dares tell them it is anything less than a joy to the palate. Few invitations are more unwelcome than one to pop in and try some peapod wine. I am afraid that I lost a few friends in those early days as the risk of coming to see me must have seemed too great. Now the mistakes are much less frequent but I do attempt new and unusual recipes from time to time and try to be painfully honest with myself and ask my guests to be painfully honest too.

Despite setbacks, glorious triumphs are often won and the home brewer soon develops a fine if small repertoire of things he or she actually likes and the best way to make them. For some it is a matter of making only one brew a year – sloe gin being a favourite in this regard and elderberry wine another. I regularly make half a dozen favourite wines and four or five beers, but I also take a more experimental approach and try to brew anything that looks remotely promising and even a few things that don't. I try exotic sugars, ancient brewing techniques and unusual fruits and plants. For example, my attempt to make milk wine was a resounding failure – imagine sweet, fizzy, sour milk with a dash of surgical spirit – but then it was bound to be. Nevertheless I learned something – in this case that you should not try to make milk wine. I also talk to people about their own experiences and have been informed and inspired by their adventures. How you pursue your home-brewing career is entirely up to you. Just remember to have fun and that you need please no one but yourself.

I hope that you will find something to please you within these pages. I cover recipes and methods that may already be familiar to you and many that you are unlikely to have come across before. Some are so new that at the time of writing I am the only person to have ever tried them – these are the fruits of my more successful experiments. On the whole I have been fairly conservative in my choice of recipes, striving for simplicity wherever possible and avoiding over-complicated or unlikely combinations. There is, for example, a recipe for dandelion wine but none for dandelion and banana wine.

There are four main types of home brewing: infusions, wines, beers and ciders. Distillation is, sadly, illegal in this country without a licence, not that this minor technicality has stopped people doing it; they just do it very quietly. Of our four available varieties of home brewing, infusions are by far the easiest to make at home. They require almost no equipment and some can be ready to drink in 24 hours or even less. Wines are considerably more complicated, and some ciders need a great deal of attention to detail if you are to end up with the type you want. Beers can often be the most difficult drinks to brew but being, to my taste at least, the easiest brews to drink are worth every last piece of effort. I use some of the old techniques for brewing beer but also some of the newer, much less time-consuming and less equipment-heavy methods.

Can you save money by brewing your own booze? Oh yes, undoubtedly. Of course, you could save even more by giving up booze altogether but that would be a flight from wisdom. Infusions will always be expensive to make because you have to buy the spirits, although you will be able to make some liqueurs much more cheaply than they would be if you bought them. However, with wines, beers and ciders the savings are substantial. A bottle of commercial blackberry wine may cost around £7, compared to just a few pennies for the homemade version. Beer, too, costs pennies a pint, surpassing by a long way even the cheapest supermarket beers. For the enthusiastic drinker this can amount to a great deal of money over a year. The true joy of this is that you are not paying the sin taxes, which, we are told, are imposed for our own good. Home brewers decide for themselves what is good for them.

Yeast bubbling contentedly

Fermentation

Brewing is an ancient art and one of the greatest achievements of man. Although there is still something magical about the process of brewing, in the past it was considered by many cultures to be *pure* magic. A sugary liquid was prepared, maybe from malted barley, grapes, berries, tree sap or apples, and left alone. Then something wonderful happened to it. The magic, we now know, comes in the form of a microscopic fungus called yeast.

Although there are many, many species of yeast it is *Saccharomyces cerevisiae*, brewer's or baker's yeast, that is of chief interest to us. And how extraordinarily interesting it is. This organism occurs naturally in several strains and many more have been developed, each with its own blend of talents for producing a variety of good flavours, reducing bad ones, tolerating high alcohol levels or low temperatures, conveniently falling to the bottom of the brew when their work is done (flocculation), and so on. These varying abilities will suit different types of brew – wine, cider and beer – helping to produce the various flavours we like.

Yeast is a microfungus, more closely related to truffles and morels than many moulds. Its cells are tiny, comparable to the size of fungal spores, at 5–10 microns across. That means 100–200 cells placed side by side would form a row 1mm long.

Yeasts feed directly on solutions of the simple sugars glucose, maltose and trehalose, and indirectly on the more complex fructose, sucrose and others, creating by-products of ethanol and carbon dioxide. Yeasts prefer to have access to oxygen but if the oxygen supply runs out they change their lifestyle and live without it.

In all brewing processes it is necessary to employ an aerobic phase (oxygen present) so that the yeast population can develop quickly, followed by an anaerobic phase (oxygen excluded, which in practice means fitting a lid or air lock to keep the air out), during which time the alcohol is created. Once the fermentable sugar runs out, or the alcohol reaches concentrations that the yeast can no longer tolerate, fermentation stops. Lack of trace nutrients can also limit yeast growth.

You need an awful lot of yeast cells to turn all the sugar in a brewing recipe into alcohol, but they reproduce asexually at an energetic pace provided the conditions are to their liking. The amount of alcohol in a finished brew is expressed in terms of the percentage of absolute alcohol by volume (ABV). If the alcohol from 100ml of a 40% ABV drink was removed there would be 40ml of it. Carbon dioxide, the other by-product of fermentation, is a bonus in most beers, some ciders and a few wines as it produces the fizzy quality we love in many of our drinks.

As well as the fermentable sugars mentioned above there are other sugars which yeasts are unable to digest – unfermentable sugars. Unfermentable sugars are left in the brew to sweeten and round the flavour. They are much more prevalent in beers than in wines and ciders.

Sugar and specific gravity

Specific gravity is of central importance in home brewing so it helps to understand what it is. The sugar content of a must or wort or apple juice (the various concoctions you start with prior to fermentation) is indicated by its specific gravity (SG), which can be measured with a hydrometer. Specific gravity is the ratio of the density of the must, wort or juice to the density of water. Water has (quite obviously if you paid attention at school) a specific gravity of 1, or 1000 as it is usually rendered.

As the sugar level in a must, wort or juice is increased the solution becomes denser and its specific gravity rises, and as the sugar is fermented out by the yeast to be replaced by alcohol, the specific gravity decreases. If, for example, you have 5 litres of must ready to be fermented into wine, and it contains 1.2kg ordinary sugar, then the original gravity (OG) will be about 1092. I say 'contains' because adding 1.2kg sugar to 5 litres water will give a different, lower, figure.

Nearly every recipe that involves fermentation will require you to keep a close eye on the specific gravity. Knowing how much sugar is in a must, juice or wort will give you a fair indication of how much alcohol will be in your finished drink.

If we fermented out the must mentioned above we would end up with a specific gravity of around 990–995 depending on a number of variables such as the type of yeast used. This is known as the final gravity (FG). Since we know how much sugar has been consumed (all of it in this instance) we know roughly how much alcohol the wine contains. Incidentally the specific gravity of the finished wine is below 1000 because alcohol has a specific gravity of less than 1000.

An approximate figure for alcohol content can be obtained from the original and final gravities, using a simple formula: (OG – FG) x 0.13. For example: (1090 – 0995) x 0.13 gives a figure of 12.4% ABV.

While it is easy to add a precise amount of sugar to a wine must, this does not necessarily result in the specific gravity you want; fruit, for example, can add or even take away sugar. It is very important therefore to test a must before fermentation and add sugar or water as needed to adjust the original gravity.

Yeasts are only able to tolerate a certain level of alcohol before they stop working. Had the amount of sugar in our must been much higher, say 1.5kg, then some sugar would have been left over. Having leftover sugar enables us to make sweet wines – there are other ways of making a sweet wine, but we will come to that in good time.

With cider it is essential to know how much sugar is in your apple juice and to add sugar or, preferably, some sweeter apple juice should it be necessary.

Beers are a little different because they contain high levels of unfermentable sugars – up to 25%. They generally have a much lower original gravity and a much higher final gravity than wines. A typical beer will start at around 1045 and finish at 1010. The fact that they finish at around 1010 indicates the existence of sugar that has not fermented out.

As well as telling you where sugar levels should start and end, specific gravity readings will indicate how things are going during fermentation and, most importantly, when fermentation has stopped. If the specific gravity remains the same for two consecutive days, then it has indeed stopped and you can proceed to the next stage.

Measuring specific gravity

A hydrometer for testing the specific gravity of alcohol is so essential a piece of kit that I keep several in my cupboard as I could not bear to go without should one get dropped. Every hydrometer is calibrated to measure the specific gravity at 20°C and if it is used at temperatures much more than a degree higher or lower it will give seriously misleading readings.

When you buy a new hydrometer it is well worth testing it in water at 20°C. The figure where the marked gauge enters the water should be 1000. If the reading is 1000 then all is well, if not then remember to add or subtract the difference in all subsequent readings; better still, send it back to the shop. Note that the water will rise up the stem of the hydrometer owing to surface tension; this should be ignored.

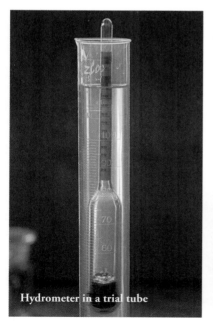

Hydrometer in a trial tube

SG read from bottom of meniscus

Cleanliness

Whatever it is you are making, things can go wrong and nearly always it is a matter of poor hygiene. The good news is that with infusions you can get away with hygiene standards that would have you closed down if you were a restaurant and still have a perfectly respectable drink at the end. The high alcohol, and sometimes sugar, levels that are used in infusions such as sloe gin protect them from all the bugs that would otherwise spoil the drink.

With wines, ciders and beers it is quite different and a great deal can go wrong quickly, easily and often irretrievably. Nearly all problems encountered in brewing can be laid at the door of contamination with one micro-organism or another. At the heart of the matter, you are trying to create the perfect conditions for micro-organisms to grow, while being extremely choosy about which one; that is, the particular strain of yeast needed for the task. With beers, unsterilised equipment is perfectly acceptable until after the boil (see p.202) but wine-making seldom involves boiling your ingredients, and everything needs to be scrupulously sterilised right from the start. Fermenting buckets, demi-johns, siphons, air locks, corks, caps, bottles and anything else that touches your brew must be sterilised.

Sterilising equipment

With the exception of infusing equipment and the buckets and pots used in the early stages of beer-making, everything used in home brewing must be sterile, so when I say something like 'Pour the wort into the fermenting bucket' just assume that I really mean 'Pour the wort into a fermenting bucket which has been cleaned and sterilised until it squeaks'.

Steam cleaning I have a domestic steam-cleaner and it works wonderfully well and very quickly, blasting away dirt with ease – though it is possible to crack glass bottles and melt polypropylene containers if you are not careful. I bought one after an unfortunate experience with a bottle of elderflower sparkly. I was about to open it when I noticed a large dark lump floating at the top. The bottle remains unopened to this day because I'm fearful of what it contains – I hope it is a lump of sediment left over from the bottle's previous contents that I failed to rinse out, but it looks awfully like a pickled shrew to me. Although it's very good at cleaning I do not trust a steam-cleaner to thoroughly sterilise my equipment. For this you need chemicals.

Chlorine-based bleach I recommend that you use this as the core of your sterilising regime. If you don't wish to use domestic bleach, chlorine-based agents are available from home-brew stores. Using 10ml bleach per 5 litres cold water is effective in killing just about everything you do not want, and it does so almost instantly.

First of all everything needs to be cleaned with weak detergent, bottle brushes and so on. Make up a batch and pour a small amount into the fermenting vessels, demi-johns or bottles immediately prior to using them. Swirl it around so that all the surfaces are sterilised. Empty the solution and rinse the containers several times to remove the chlorine smell. It is quickly rinsed away if you avoid the viscous varieties of bleach and stick to the cheap watery stuff. It is well worth using a dilute solution of sodium metabisulphite (1 tsp in 1 litre water) for the second rinse as it neutralises the smell of the chlorine – and is a sterilising agent itself.

Hydrogen peroxide This is another excellent sterilising agent. Content as I am with bleach, I have never used it but would nevertheless recommend it based on the experience of others. At the very low concentrations you will be using, it will be perfectly safe and has the advantage over bleach of having no smell at all. Follow the instructions on the packaging, make up a solution and swirl around the inside of your demi-johns, fermenters, bottles and so on. Rinse with tap water.

Sodium metabisulphite Although not quite so powerful as the two chemicals above, sodium metabisulphite can be employed on its own as a steriliser. I use it just for awkward things like siphons, air locks and corks. It can be bought cheaply in crystalline form.

When taking the lid off the container, do not be tempted to sniff the contents – it will literally take your breath away because the sulphur dioxide it gives off turns to sulphuric acid in your respiratory system and can cause an asthma attack in susceptible individuals.

The normal concentration used is 2 tsp per litre. Always make a fresh solution every time you use it as the sulphur dioxide soon escapes. Soak the items to be sterilised in the solution for a few minutes, then rinse with tap water. As noted above it is excellent at neutralising the odour of chlorine.

Cleaning and sterilising bottles

Bottles used for infusions simply need to be clean, not sterile. However, wine, cider and beer bottles need to be completely sterile otherwise any number of nasty things can happen. Both reused and new bottles need to be sterilised.

The only drawback with second-hand bottles is the old labels. The best way to remove them is to leave the bottles in a bin or bath full of water for 2 days then peel off the labels. The glue comes away easily with coarse wire scouring pads.

Rinse the bottles with hot water, then part-fill one of them with a solution of bleach (see p.16), place a funnel in another bottle and transfer the solution. Continue until all the bottles have been treated. Drain the solution from the bottles as much as possible. The solution lasts for about two dozen bottles – any more and a fresh solution should be used. Now perform the same process using first hot water, then a solution of sodium metabisulphite (1 tsp in 500ml hot water), then hot water again, shaking the fluids in the bottle at each stage.

One thing that used to cause me perpetual annoyance was the impossibility of draining every last drop of cleaning fluid and rinsing water from my washed bottles. Then I came across a bottle tree (pictured right) and my life was complete.

Keeping everything covered

Finally, even if everything is clean, it is possible, in fact likely, that airborne bugs will find their way into your brew if it is left uncovered. One particularly nasty aerial menace is the vinegar fly, also known as the fruit fly. My difficult relationship with this tiny organism began when my mother, unable to face telling me the facts of life, bought me an equally shy book, which unhelpfully explained matters of a delicate nature by talking at length about fruit flies (they have very large chromosomes, don't you know?). I was confused for decades. Now that damn thing has come back to haunt me by flying into my brews bearing various bacteria which turn my brews to vinegar. The moral of this story is to always keep your demi-johns air-locked and your fermenting buckets covered with a lid, and to tell children the truth.

Keeping records

This is a fine case of asking people to 'do as I say, not as I do', for I am an appalling record-keeper. But it is truly worth the effort. If something comes out too sweet, too flat, too sharp or just terrible, your records will enable you to avoid the mistake in future. You should write down everything you do to provide you with a good record of how the brew was made. Ingredients and their quantities, timings, specific gravities, temperatures, tastes – everything you can think of should be recorded. I have several notebooks (only because I keep mislaying them) with reasonable records contained therein and they have been invaluable. But do try to be better at this than I am.

A rather obvious but important part of record keeping is to *put labels on things*. I was not very good at that either but as the number of demi-johns and subsequent wine bottles of unknown contents grew I realised that things must change. Even though you think you will never forget what that demi-john contains I promise that you will. I still have countless bottles of wine labelled 'Parsnip??' or 'Gorse??' – don't let that happen to you. The big turn-around for me was the purchase of a label printer, which is attached to my computer. Now I can print out dozens of identical labels with ease.

Bottle-drying tree

Adding hops at copper-up

Essential terms

Aeration Introducing air into a (usually) unfermented brew by whisking or stirring to provide oxygen for primary fermentation of yeast.

Air lock A plastic or glass device which allows carbon dioxide to escape from a fermentation while not permitting air to enter.

Alpha acids A component of hops, which after boiling impart bitterness to beer.

Autolysis The decomposition of dead yeast, generally producing off-flavours but sometimes beneficial.

Base malt The malt, usually pale ale, used in beer-making to provide the bulk of the sugars in a wort.

Campden tablet A measured amount of sodium metabisulphite in tablet form.

Cheese A construction of pomace and straw used in traditional presses to filter out the juice in cider-making.

Cold-sparge To pass cold water through the used beer hops when liquoring down.

Conditioning The continued fermentation of a brew, generally in a sealed container so that the carbon dioxide produced is retained in solution under pressure.

Copper finings A substance added to the boil to help clear a beer.

Copper-up In beer-making, the moment when the wort begins to boil.

Demi-john A container with a narrow neck in which wines and ciders may be fermented, typically 4.5 litres capacity.

Diacetyl A chemical which produces a strong flavour of butter in a brew.

Diacetyl rest A period when the temperature of a beer is increased slightly to enable yeast to absorb and thus remove diacetyl.

Diastatic power The power of the enzymes in a malted grain to convert starches into sugars.

Home brewer's calendar

 In season

	JAN		FEB		MARCH		APRIL		MAY	
Alexanders	■	■	■	■	■	■	■	■		
Birch Sap					■	■				
Blackberry										
Blackthorn Leaves									■	■
Brooklime									■	■
Cherry										
Cherry Plum										
Cowslip							■	■	■	
Crab Apple										
Damson										
Dandelion					■	■	■	■	■	
Elderberry										
Elderflower										
Fennel									■	■
Gooseberry										
Gorse	■	■	■	■	■	■	■	■	■	■
Green Walnut										
Haws										
Japanese Rose Petals										
Japanese Rosehip										
Mugwort									■	■
Primrose					■	■	■	■		
Raspberry										
Rhubarb					■	■	■	■	■	■
Sea Buckthorn										
Sloe										
Strawberry										
Sweet Chestnut										
Sweet Cicely									■	■
Sweet Vernal Grass									■	■
Watermint							■	■	■	■
Wild Rosehip										
Wormwood									■	■

A guide to the best times to prepare wines and infusions from seasonal ingredients.

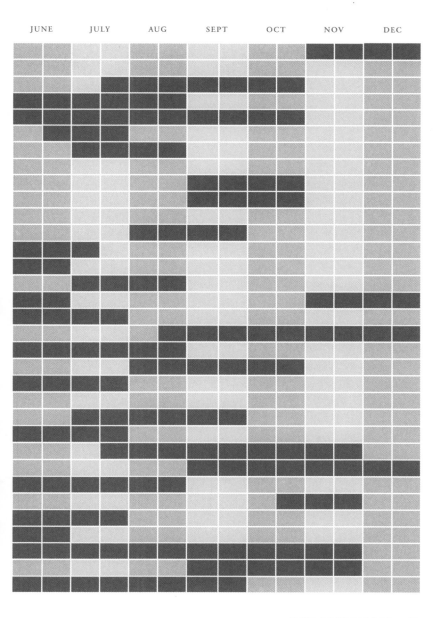

Infusions

In this country we live under a partly sensible law that forbids us

to distil alcohol. But while homemade whisky, vodka, gin and rum are off the home-brew menu there is really nothing to stop us modifying the flavour of shop-bought spirits in whatever way we choose. Enter, if you please, the wonderful world of infusions.

I am a big infusion enthusiast and few items of vegetable matter have escaped my infuser's hand. That is the exciting thing about it – if you like the taste of a plant, fruit, nut, or just about anything that is at least partly soluble in water or alcohol and *not* poisonous, then you can make an infusion out of it. Endless experimentation is possible as the process is always easy, often very quick indeed and, unlike beers and wines, infusions can be made in tiny quantities. If you like melons or kumquats, fennel or bay, chestnuts or walnuts, just drop them in alcohol for a while to see if you like the resulting liquor.

Types of infusion

There are four kinds of infusions: fruit, nut, floral and plant.

Fruit infusions As a dedicated forager I come across endless amounts of fruit from the hedgerow every year. Some, like raspberries and blackberries, find ready use in the kitchen but many are a trial for the cook. I cannot, however, think of any *edible* wild fruit that does not make a good infusion and otherwise intractable fruits, such as sloes, elderberries and rosehips, make themselves useful at last.

Of course the hedgerow is not for everyone, but fruits from the garden, shop or market are just as infusible, although even the most reluctant forager might find it depressing to buy blackberries. Like hedgerow fruits, nearly any small shop-bought or home-grown fruit will work in an infusion. Whichever fruit you use, do select only those that are in perfect condition and choose fruit which is under-ripe rather than over-ripe to ensure a sharp fruitiness.

Not everything works though. Strawberry vodka, for example, is sickly, syrupy stuff and one is not encouraged by the fact that the colour leaches from the strawberries, leaving them pale, pink and looking like a bottle of shaved rats.

There is one enormous bonus with fruit infusions – you can, usually, eat the fruit after the drink is decanted off. Raspberries, damsons, cherries and many more fruits that have been gently soaking in sugar and alcohol for half a year make wonderful additions to fruit salads or trifles.

The process for making fruit infusions is so simple that the word 'process' is overstating the matter. You simply put all the ingredients into a jar, leave them, then strain out the fruit.

Nut infusions These are very popular, with several brands commercially available. It can take several months for the flavour to leave the nut and enter the alcohol, but it is worth the wait if you like nut liqueurs. Heat, however, does speed things up a little and I have occasionally resorted to standing jars of hazelnuts or macadamia nuts in warm water for a few hours to get things going.

Since the principle is very straightforward I have included only one recipe – chestnut liqueur. There is no reason why hazelnuts, walnuts, almonds, pecans and so on could not be used, although I would draw the line at peanuts. Hazelnut liqueur is the most successful as it has a good, strong flavour, almonds less so. While chestnuts are best left whole, the other nuts should be crushed. Crushed nuts produce a murky concoction, but it will clear completely if left peacefully on a shelf for a month or two before decanting into a bottle.

Floral infusions These lovely infusions are very quick and very easy. Drinking them straight can be like downing a bottle of eau de cologne, but in a mix they work very well and are certainly worth the small effort they take to make. They are also the quickest of all home brews, the bouquet of any petal being absorbed by the alcohol in a matter of hours. Not all flowers smell nice and many, such as foxglove and aconite, are actually deadly so I stick with a handful of fragrant flowers which I know are safe.

There is no need to add sugar to a floral infusion unless you want to, or you are using a very large quantity of petals that will contain sufficient water to dilute the alcohol. For this reason I have provided no proper recipes – you simply pack a Kilner jar about half-full with petals and top up with a spirit; 2 tsp sugar may be added if you want it sweetened slightly. Decanting can usually be done the next day and certainly within a week and there should be no need to filter.

Plant infusions By plant infusions, I mean everything apart from the flower, fruit or nut which is actually edible, or at least not poisonous. When picking wild plants *always* check with a plant book if you are unsure exactly what a plant looks like as some look-alikes are famously poisonous. Generally speaking, you will not need to add sugar to plants as their water content is unlikely to be great enough to seriously dilute the alcohol. Like flower infusions, most are ready very quickly, requiring only 3 or 4 days in the cupboard prior to decanting.

Since there are several hundred thousand species of plants there is an awful lot to explore – several can be bought or grown, but many are available in the hedgerow, field and wood. I have also included two recipes for which the term 'plant infusion' is stretching the definition of plant a little too far; one is made from a lichen, the other from amber. In an act of charity I have not included my recipe for seaweed gin.

Ingredients

There are only three main ingredients needed for infusions – and often you will get away with just two:

- The fruit, nut, flower or plant you wish to infuse
- A spirit, such as whisky, gin or vodka
- Sugar (sometimes optional)

Spirit Which spirit you choose to use for an infusion is entirely up to you, though vodka is the most reliable because of its neutral flavour, followed by gin, white rum and brandy. Whisky is harder to use, although there is at least one first-class drink that can be made with it; see Blackberry whisky, p.45. For the purist the spirit should, perhaps, be an eau de vie. These are unmatured distillations from grain, grape or apple fermentations.

How good a quality should your spirit be? This really depends on the strength of flavour of the infused plant material and the depth of your pocket. With fruits you can get away with supermarket own brand if you want, but for delicate flavours such as those of flowers I suggest splashing out on something a little better as the harsh qualities found in cheap liquor can overwhelm them.

Sugar Adding sugar to an infusion is not always necessary, but with most fruits, and some plants and nuts, the amount of water they will add to the liquor can dilute it to the point where things start to ferment and go bad. Sugar restores the preservative balance (osmotic pressure and stuff) and bugs will not grow. Soft fruits such as raspberries need a lot of sugar, while firmer fruits like crab apples and sloes need less. I always use granulated sugar for my infusions.

If you add sugar to an infusion the result will be a liqueur; if you do not it will remain a liquor or spirit.

Before we proceed I must come clean about my own opinion on liqueurs, if not flavoured liquors. I was brought up in Portsmouth (correctly pronounced 'paws-muff'), an interesting town but not one known for its sophistication. Should I ever have asked for a Drambuie or a Cointreau in the Fawcett Inn (seriously) eyebrows would have been raised and there would have been a very good chance I would have had to defend my masculinity in the street outside. Perhaps it is for this reason or perhaps just a general dislike of too much sweetness in alcoholic beverages that I have never had much time for certain liqueurs. But I still make them because my friends like them and some fruit liqueurs are perfectly pleasant by virtue of their intense fruitiness. And they do not always have to be sickly sweet. In addition, and this is important, sweet infusions can form the basis of a good cocktail.

Equipment

Very little equipment is required to make infusions. It all needs to be clean but nothing needs to be sterilised:

* Kitchen scales
* A 1-litre measuring jug
* Funnel
* Glass containers to infuse in. Kilner jars are the favourite, but old jam jars are also fine.
* Glass bottles to store the finished drink. Swing-top bottles are the obvious option but it is sometimes more interesting to use corked bottles. I scour junk shops and antique markets for ancient or unusual bottles and have an APB out among my friends for such treasures.

That's it, though the following may also be useful:

* Sieve
* Muslin
* Wine filter for infusions that come out cloudy

Things to consider

There is really nothing that can go wrong with infusions, even if you try. The only problem I have encountered (it was someone else, not me!) was when a cherry plum brandy started to ferment and go a little mouldy. The liquor had absorbed water from the fruit, lowering its alcohol and sugar content to levels that allowed yeasts and other micro-organisms to grow. The answer is to use relatively high levels of alcohol and sugar, or to put it another way, a relatively small amount of fruit.

Sunlight is never beneficial to alcoholic drinks; the bright attractive colours of many infusions are quickly lost and the flavour too can suffer. Always keep your infusions in a cupboard or dark corner of the kitchen.

Although it makes little difference with many infusions, leaving something to infuse for a very long time can cause cloudiness and extract some of the more unpleasant flavours. This is the voice of sad experience as I am a forgetful infuser who occasionally comes across murky bottles of orange peel that have been infusing for years rather than the required few days.

Filtering using specialist wine filter paper can reduce cloudiness. My answer to anyone who complains is to say that it is supposed to be like that.

Sloe gin (or vodka)

SEASON	September–December
INFUSION TIME	3 months–1 year

This recipe is the basis for most infusions so it is well worth reading through even if sloe gin is not for you (though why that would be so I cannot imagine). Sugar quantities and timings vary between recipes.

This famous drink is made in startlingly large quantities in the countryside. Indeed the very mention of home brewing in West Dorset during a dinner party will result in the appearance from a distant cupboard of some of this year's, last year's or autumn 1982's vintage. Opinions are sought and recipes swapped. Arguments sometimes ensue.

What is seldom discussed is where the sloes were found. This would be as socially unacceptable as discussing bank balances or marital details – foraging locations are always kept a secret. Such secrecy in most parts of the countryside is rather misplaced when it comes to sloes, as the blackthorn on which they grow is extremely common; it is just a matter of form I suppose. In town, however, blackthorn bushes are thinly distributed and a trip to the country (to steal some of ours) may be necessary.

When a blackthorn is found in fruit it tends to be in fruit a lot – the sloes cluster around the branches like long, thin bunches of grapes and a single bush will often supply the needs of a whole year. They are easy enough to pick provided you avoid the astonishingly nasty spines (it is not called *Prunus spinosa* – the 'spiny plum' – for nothing). These frequently leave you with a wound that turns septic.

If you've never tasted a raw sloe I do recommend trying one (few will wish to try more). These are among the most astringent of all fruits, resulting in comical facial distortions and un-ladylike spitting. A warm autumn and a mild early winter will often produce relatively large fruit which have turned at least some of their astringency to sweetness, but not so much that you would want to eat them for dessert.

Sloes have a chequered alcoholic history and sloe gin has only fairly recently achieved respectability as a bona-fide beverage. A few lines from a lengthy polemical poem on British ills from 1717 sums up the situation:

White, Claret, Sherry, Mountain, Tort,
Tho' none oft e'er had cross'd the Seas,
Or from the Grape deriv'd its Lees,
But made at Home, 'twixt Chip and Dash,
Of Sugar, Sloes, and Grocer's Trash

In an 1838 novel by one Edward L. Joseph, sloe juice and gin was described, scathingly, as a mixture '*which the inhabitants of London swallow for port*'. It was not until the beginning of the twentieth century that sloe gin became a respectable drink. Now everyone – well, pretty much everyone in West Dorset at least – makes it and is proud.

There seems to be a fundamental law of nature that the number of possible recipes and opportunities for argument is inversely proportional to the number of ingredients. With only three, sloe gin has accrued more recipes and opinions than any other drink I know. One of the several matters over which there is endless discussion is when the sloes should be picked.

Some pick their sloes early in the autumn but many insist on waiting until after the first frost when they become a little sweeter and the skins become softer; thus permitting the infusion, it is thought, to proceed faster. I just pick them when they are big enough. The sweetness of the fruit is immaterial in sloe gin as so much sugar is added in the making.

My advice is to just pick any sloe you find which is actually ripe, which can be from September through until Christmas. I frequently hear the suggestion that sloes should be put in the freezer for a day or two to replicate the effects of frost, but this, like the habit of pricking the fruit, just adds an extra step with little effect on the finished product.

What truly makes a difference with sloe gin is how long you leave the sloes in the gin before bottling and (the hardest part) how long you leave the bottle on the shelf before you drink it. While sloe gin is perfectly palatable after 3 months, a further year of maturity helps enormously. By a very long way the best sloe gin I have ever tasted was one made by my friend David who found a seventeen-year-old bottle in his cupboard. It was like the finest Malmsey Madeira and, crucially, tasted nothing like sloes or indeed gin. Since that happy discovery we have taken a tiny glass together every Christmas.

Why sloe gin in the bottle improves with age is a matter for the chemist but the effect on flavour from lengthening the period of infusion is easily explained. At the heart of every sloe is a stone and at the heart of every stone is a nut. The nut is a tiny version of a related but larger-fruited species, the almond. When sloes are left in the gin for 4 months to a year the flavour of almonds is extracted from the nut and permeates the drink. Of course it is all a matter of taste and it was certainly not to the taste of a country-show judge who disgracefully marked down another friend's sloe gin to second place in a competition because it tasted of almonds. If, for reasons best known to yourself, you agree with the judge then take out the sloes at around 3 months.

My basic sloe gin recipe is extremely simple; no added flavourings such as juniper berries or almonds, just straight in the jar with all three basic ingredients. Actually there is one very big thing I do differently – I prefer to use vodka. It gives a cleaner flavour and is palatable sooner than when using gin.

Makes about 600ml
280g ripe sloes, washed
140g sugar
About 600ml gin or vodka

Put the sloes in a 1-litre Kilner jar, pour over the sugar and the gin, close the lid and shake. Store the jar in a dark cupboard, shaking once every day until the sugar has all dissolved.

After 3 months – or 6 months or a year – strain out the sloes, using a muslin-lined funnel placed in a bottle. Cork or seal your bottle and store in a dark cupboard. Wait for at least a year before drinking... if you can.

If your sloe gin is a little murky it is possible to filter out the offending particles using filter paper placed in a funnel. Buy some good-quality wine filter papers (coffee filter paper does not work) and fold them repeatedly to form a pleated cone.

Slider

I cannot leave sloe gin without mentioning the dark subject of slider. This is a drink devised to avoid the unhappy experience of having to throw away used sloes, which people know in their hearts to still contain a certain amount of flavour, sugar, and most importantly, alcohol.

Attempts have been made to remove the stones from sloes and dip the flesh in chocolate, something I have tried myself. You might as well dip little bits of softened leather in chocolate, it will taste better.

Much more sensible is to chuck the whole lot into some dry cider to make what is in effect a reverse infusion. The resulting, somewhat strangely coloured, liquor (it looks like a slightly brown rosé) has the flavour that one would expect – fruity, almondy and cidery. Slider acquired its name partly from a rather obvious play on words, but mostly from making people slide down the wall they find themselves leaning against.

The easiest way to make slider is to simply top up your Kilner jar of sloes with dry still cider after you have decanted off the sloe gin. It is worth drinking within a couple of weeks as the exposure to the air can spoil the cider and even start it fermenting again. A variation is to use a dry wine (white or red) instead of cider but it is difficult to know what to call it. 'Sline' is not an appealing name for anything you would want to drink.

Smoked sloe gin (or vodka)

SEASON	All year
INFUSION TIME	Not applicable

This is a silly idea but I have had an enormous amount of fun with it. We are used to eating smoked foods and some of us even smoke food at home. In fact hot-smoking fish on a grid over a frying pan of oak chips, cinnamon, cloves, etc. is easy and I highly recommend it. But what of smoked sloe gin or smoked drinks in general? Is it easy to smoke alcoholic drinks, and why would you want to?

Well, it is very easy; I have been experimenting and have devised a set-up you can cobble together in 10 minutes from stuff lying around the kitchen. As to 'why', I must really leave that for you to answer when you try it, but there is a noticeable effect on flavour and it looks so very cool.

Smoking drinks is simply a matter of squirting smoke through a drink, any drink, and serving immediately. If you get it just right there is a little bit of smoke floating above the liquor in the glass. For this you will need a saucepan you do not think too highly of and a scrupulously clean, used squirty washing-up-liquid bottle, with a small plastic or metal tube pushed into the nozzle.

Smoking is a worthwhile excursion for some drinks but certainly not for others. It goes well with highly flavoured, rather heavy tipples – I certainly would not recommend trying it with elderflower sparkly or cowslip wine, but with sloe gin, whisky and seriously heavy beers such as my Rauchbier (p.228) it does work.

Makes 2 glasses
2 glasses of sloe gin or vodka (p.35)
½ cup of oak chips
Pared zest of ½ orange
1 cinnamon stick
About 6 cloves

Have your glasses of sloe gin ready. Place all the other ingredients in your oldest saucepan and fashion a foil tent with a little closed chimney over the top. Set it over a medium heat. Once smoke starts to creep under the edge of the tent, just snip the point of the chimney off with scissors, quickly suck out some of the smoke with the washing-up-liquid bottle and immediately inject it into the glasses of sloe gin. One squirt usually does the trick though you can do it again if you like. Serve absolutely immediately.

Damson vodka

SEASON	September–October; July–August for cherry plums
INFUSION TIME	3 months

Large plums are difficult to use for infusions because they tend to rot before they are permeated with sufficient sugar and alcohol to preserve them, and cutting plums in half will just make the drink cloudy. But small plums, particularly damsons, work extremely well in an infusion, like their sloe relatives.

Damsons are naturally palatable and damson gin or vodka is likewise palatable and much more quickly so than the sloe equivalent, as the fruit lacks the tannin that gives the latter its astringency. Wild damsons are found in late summer/early autumn but since the fruit is only locally abundant most people will rely on home-grown or the shop for their supply.

If you are a keen forager you should consider the cherry plum. These, as their name suggests, are plums that look like cherries (not the other way round). They are increasingly common these days, as beneficent highway authorities have taken to planting them along roadsides. They are highly conspicuous because of the enormous number of colourful fruit they produce for several weeks during high summer.

Both red and yellow varieties are found, with orange fruit seen on rare occasions. Nevertheless people often pass them by as unknowns, to fall on the pavement in a squashy mess. Like all plums, the quality of the fruit varies from tree to tree and year to year with no clue as to what one will taste like from appearance alone. Sometimes they are quite bland so make sure you select those which are fruity or even a little under-ripe.

Makes about 600ml
280g damsons or cherry plums
140g sugar
About 600ml vodka

Put the damsons or cherry plums and sugar in a 1-litre Kilner jar, top up with vodka nearly to the brim, close the lid and shake. Store in a dark cupboard, shaking once every day until the sugar has all dissolved.

Decant the liqueur from the plums after 3 months and bottle. Allow to mature for a year or so before drinking. Eat the plums with ice cream.

Sea buckthorn vodka

SEASON	Late July–November
INFUSION TIME	3 months

Like cherry plums, sea buckthorn is frequently planted along roadsides as a hardy small tree. This willow-like plant is native to Britain; at least it is native to the south-eastern coasts. As well as roadsides, it has frequently been planted in coastal locations to fix dunes. Unfortunately it likes sand dunes a little too much and will quickly engulf existing vegetation with a dense thicket of sea buckthorn, much to the consternation of conservationists. Where it is growing as an invasive species it is a gift to the forager who can take whatever he or she wants with a clear conscience.

But what is it that grows on sea buckthorn that should so interest the home brewer? It is the densely packed, bright orange berries. These have a flavour halfway between orange juice and battery acid, but you must not let this put you off. In an infusion the acidity is kept to moderate levels and it makes a fruity, sweet drink which is great in mixes.

The berries form in late July/early August and can be picked from then until November. The main problem is picking them intact, as they are little balloons of juice which pop with the slightest squeeze. The answer I am afraid is to just pick very carefully and, if you feel justified in doing so, cutting off a complete branch and dealing with them at home. Be warned, however: the branches have vicious spines which, like blackthorn, inflict septic wounds.

The recipe is the same as for sloe gin except, of course, you should use vodka. It is extremely fruity, nicely offsetting the sweetness. I like it with soda water and ice or, best of all, in a sparkling elderflower cocktail.

Makes about 250ml
170g sea buckthorn berries
100g sugar
About 250ml vodka

Put the sea buckthorn berries and sugar in a 500ml Kilner jar, top up with vodka, close the lid and shake. Store in a dark cupboard, shaking once every day until the sugar has all dissolved.

Strain the infused vodka from the berries after 3 months and bottle. Leave to mature for 3 months before drinking.

Rosehip vodka

SEASON	August–November
INFUSION TIME	4 months

Foragers hate to let anything go to waste and the abundant rosehip is a temptation not to be resisted. It is not the easiest of fruits to use in the kitchen because of the dangerously hairy seeds nestling inside, but rosehip vodka avoids such perils, as the stomach-irritating seeds remain safely where they are. Like most other children of my generation I was brought up on a daily spoonful of rosehip syrup by way of apology for the daily dose of cod liver oil. What my mother never gave me was rosehip vodka; I guess she kept that for herself.

Any rosehip from any rose – garden or wild – will work, though the gigantic hips of the Japanese rose are likely to rot before they make a good infusion unless you pick them while they are still very firm. Rosehips come in two varieties – under-ripe and over-ripe but never, it seems, ripe. With small hips it does not matter which you use. Made to the same recipe as sloe gin, but with a little less sugar, the flavour is surprisingly fruity with a distinct note of vanilla.

Makes about 600ml
300g firm rosehips
120g sugar
About 600ml vodka

Place the rosehips and sugar in a 1-litre Kilner jar, top up with the vodka, close the lid and shake. Store in a dark cupboard, shaking once a day until the sugar has dissolved.

Decant the infused vodka from the rosehips after 4 months and bottle. Allow to mature for 3 months before drinking.

Blackberry whisky

SEASON	Late July–October
INFUSION TIME	6 months

While most people are wary of picking wild berries, no one is the least concerned about picking blackberries. The fruit is super-abundant in all but the most urban of locations and even in the city it can often be found in overgrown parks and gardens and on wasteland. It is the first foraged food we ever learn about and sadly often the only one.

Endless quantities are available from late July to the end of October – I must have picked nearly a ton in my lifetime. Do not worry about the ancient advice to not pick blackberries after Michaelmas (11th October) when the Devil spits on them. This is a reference to the grey mould that infects the fruit, which is more common as the year progresses. Provided they look good they are perfectly edible.

Blackberry whisky is one of the finest of all infusions, a rival even to sloe gin. Do use cheap whisky for this recipe as there is a special pit in hell for those who drink good whisky in any way other than on its own.

For those few who do not like blackberries and the many more who do not like whisky I have some good news. Given time – about a year, but two is better – the flavour mellows into something quite its own, not dissimilar from port, and with never a hint of peat bogs and barely a trace of blackberry crumble.

I have dispensed with weights here as volumes guide this recipe.

Blackberries
Sugar
Whisky

Two-thirds fill a Kilner jar with blackberries, then sprinkle sugar over them until it covers the bottom half of the fruit. The blackberries should be dry for this operation otherwise the sugar will not flow. Top up the jar with whisky, close the lid and shake gently. Store in a dark cupboard and shake once a day until the sugar has dissolved.

After 6 months, decant the infused whisky into a bottle and store for at least a year to mature. The sweet whisky-soaked blackberries are quite delicious so do not throw them away!

Raspberry vodka

SEASON	July–September
INFUSION TIME	3 months

Few foraging pleasures are more intense than standing in a woodland glade picking a handful of raspberries and popping the lot into your mouth. It is as unfussy a dining experience as you could imagine and difficult to beat. Since this is the only sensible way to eat wild raspberries, cultivated varieties will be required to make an infusion.

Raspberries are the ideal infusible fruit, possessing a perfect balance of subtle flavours and acidity. An eau de vie could be used instead of vodka and I suggest for once that if vodka is used it should not be of the cheap, harsh variety as this will compromise the delicate flavour of the fruit.

Makes about 600ml
280g raspberries
140g sugar
About 600ml vodka or eau de vie

Place the raspberries in a 1-litre Kilner jar and add the sugar. Top up with vodka, close the lid and shake. Store in a dark cupboard, shaking once a day until all the sugar has dissolved.

Decant the infused vodka into a bottle after 3 months, then leave it to mature for 6 months before drinking. The sweet vodka-soaked raspberries are particularly good so don't share.

Haw gin

SEASON	Late August–early December
INFUSION TIME	3 months

By a long way, the haw is the commonest fruit growing in our hedgerows. Hawthorn trees were planted on an industrial scale during the various periods of enclosure, but especially in the nineteenth century. While the hawthorn forms an excellent, stock-proof hedge it is a pity that its fruit is not a little more exciting.

The humble haw consists of a large pip surrounded by a thin layer of soft, almost tasteless flesh and a dull red skin. Various techniques have been devised to use this bounteous if slightly disappointing fruit, the best being a crab apple and haw fruit leather. However, it does make an excellent sherry-like infusion. This recipe was supplied by my herbalist friend Monica, who tells me that it is also terribly good for you – keeping your blood pressure under control and strengthening cardiovascular action. All without getting out of your armchair.

Makes about 250ml

Sufficient ripe haws to fill a 500ml Kilner jar

2 tsp sugar, more if you want it sweeter

About 250ml gin

Loosely pack the haws into your 500ml Kilner jar, sprinkling the sugar between the layers. Top up with gin, seal the lid and shake to dissolve the sugar. Store in a dark cupboard and shake once a day.

Decant the infused gin into bottles after 3 months. The haws will have lost their dusky pink coloration and turned the gin the colour of rosé. Leave to mature for a year or so before drinking.

Crab apple eau de vie

SEASON	September–October
INFUSION TIME	6 months

Because they are so large it is near impossible to make an infusion of even the smallest cultivated apple as they would simply rot away to form a nasty brown mess. However the small size of crab apples and their disinclination to rot even under extreme provocation make them perfect for the job. The hedgerows abound with apples that sometimes pass for crab apples because they grow wild. Most of these will be 'wildings' – apple trees grown from discarded cores and bearing fruit with near random characteristics.

True crab apples are more often found in old woodland and hedges and produce rock-hard and highly acidic fruit made almost entirely of skin and pips surrounded by membranes with a toenail-like texture, perfect, in other words, for an infusion. It takes at least 6 months to thoroughly extract the apple flavour. This is one of my favourite wild infusions as the flavour is intensely and cleanly of apple.

Apple eau de vie is not commonly seen in the shops, but Julian Temperley of the Somerset Distillery makes it and deserves a knighthood for reviving the lost art of distilling fermented apple juice in Britain.

Makes about 600ml
280g small crab apples
140g sugar
About 600ml apple eau de vie
    (vodka will do, but it's not as good)

Put the crab apples and sugar in a 1-litre Kilner jar and top up nearly to the brim with apple eau de vie (or vodka). The apples will float partly out of the liquor so scrunch up a small amount of foil and place it on top of the apples to hold them under. Close the lid and shake. Store in a dark cupboard and shake gently once a day until all the sugar has dissolved.

Decant the infused liquor into bottles after 6 months. Leave to mature for a year or so before drinking.

Cherry brandy

SEASON	Late June–July
INFUSION TIME	2–6 months

Although there is no reason why other alcohols could not be used, brandy is the obvious choice for a cherry infusion. Cherries are sometimes found in the wild, or more likely, semi-wild as a planted roadside tree. July is the best time to dangerously scan the hedgerows as you drive along. However, they are not always easy to find, so most people will rely on fruit from their garden or the market.

Cherry brandy tastes better if the fruit is removed fairly quickly – within a couple of months. If you leave it longer the almond flavour is extracted from the stone and your cherry brandy will taste inescapably like the disgusting syrupy, pink medicine I gave my young daughters when they were feeling unwell. The alternative is to remove the stone first, though the drink may be a little cloudy as the exposed flesh is carried into the liquor. Of course you may like the almond flavour, in which case leave the cherries in for 6 months. Recipes for cherry brandy go back to at least the eighteenth century and some even suggest making a liqueur from the stones alone – the cherries themselves being eaten – to give a strongly almond-flavoured drink.

Makes about 600ml
**300g cherries (traditionally black
 cherries, but any will do)
120g sugar
About 600ml brandy**

Put the cherries, stoned or not, into a 1-litre Kilner jar, add the sugar and top up with brandy. Close the lid and shake. Store in a dark cupboard and shake once a day until all the sugar has dissolved.

Decant the infused brandy into bottles through a muslin-lined funnel at 2 months (or 6 months if you prefer an almondy flavour). Allow to mature for a year or so before drinking.

Orange liqueur

SEASON	All year
INFUSION TIME	1–7 days

While sloe gin and most other fruit infusions take months to develop their flavour, orange liqueur is ready in a day. The resulting liqueur is like the famous Cointreau.

A rather pretty alternative is kumquat vodka, which needs at least twice as much sugar as the fruit contains a lot of water. This drink, or something very much like it, is a favourite in Corfu.

Orange liqueurs are good on their own but much better in a long drink made with, well, orange juice. Pour a shot or two of the liqueur into a glass, pour on fresh orange juice, stir and add crushed ice.

Makes about 350ml
**1 orange, unwaxed and as shiny and
    fresh as possible
1 tbsp sugar
350ml vodka**

Use a potato peeler to slice off the zest of an orange, pop it into a 350ml Kilner jar, sprinkle on the sugar and top up with vodka. Close the lid and shake until the sugar has dissolved. Place in a dark cupboard and shake once a day.

Remove the peel after no more than a week as the liqueur can become cloudy. If you want to drink it immediately then it can be ready in half an hour if you warm the jar in hot water.

Variation

Lemon liqueur Simply replace the orange with lemon zest. This will find many a use as a cocktail ingredient or simply with soda, lemon juice and crushed ice as an alcoholic lemonade.

Pomegranate rum

SEASON	All year
INFUSION TIME	3 months

The first time my mother gave me a pomegranate to eat I thought she was playing a cruel joke. Although the flavour was quite pleasant it clearly was not an edible fruit because of the absurd number of pips. An aunt of mine lived long under the mistaken impression that I liked the damn things and would bring me one every time she visited. I hate them. However, pips are no hindrance if you want to make a liqueur and the fact that the pomegranate makes such a fine one is no surprise when you consider that the essential ingredient in many a cocktail is grenadine – pomegranate cordial. If you use pomegranate rum as grenadine you will be adding extra alcohol to your cocktail, but I will not judge you.

Makes about 250ml
1 pomegranate
50g sugar
About 250ml white rum

Carefully break open the pomegranate and gently tease apart the arils (the proper name for the seeds and their surrounding juice pockets). Place these in a 500ml Kilner jar, taking care to exclude the bitter membranes. Add the sugar and top up with rum. Close the lid and shake. Store in a dark cupboard and shake once a day until the sugar has dissolved.

Decant the infused rum into bottles after 3 months. Leave to mature for a year or so before drinking. This really is one of the best infusions I know, with a pleasant bitter bite. I highly recommend that you try it.

Chestnut liqueur

SEASON	Mid October–November
INFUSION TIME	3 months

I would not sit and drink a glass of chestnut liqueur neat, as the flavour is rather cloying, but it makes an excellent base for a cocktail with a soft ginger beer or soda water. The chief problem with it is that the resultant infusion tends to cloudiness, which either has to be tolerated or removed by careful filtration.

The best chestnuts I ever saw were in Piedmont, while on a British Mycological Society visit. We were distracted from our mycological pursuits one morning by a vast chestnut coppice, the floor of which was covered in fat, ripe chestnuts. This would never happen in Britain. Our native sweet chestnuts ripen, if they ripen at all, in mid-October, though few trees produce useful fruit and those that do bestow nuts that are seldom more than a quarter the size of their continental cousins. Unless you are very lucky you will simply have to buy your chestnuts from the shop.

Unfortunately chestnuts need to be peeled. To do this, boil them for 12 minutes then turn off the heat, leaving the chestnuts in the hot water. Don one rubber glove, take the chestnuts one at a time from the pan and cut a fairly wide slit on the flat side from the pointy end. Grab hold of the skin of the flat side and carefully peel it away, trying to peel the inner skin with it. Peel away the rest of the skin. This works much better on really fresh chestnuts, so buy early in the season if you can.

Makes about 600ml
280g peeled sweet chestnuts
150g sugar
About 600ml rum, vodka or brandy

Place the chestnuts and sugar in a 1-litre Kilner jar and top up with your spirit of choice. Close the lid and shake. Store in a dark cupboard and very gently shake the jar once a day until the sugar has dissolved.

After 3 months decant the liqueur into bottles, filtering if necessary. The chestnuts can be added to a fruit cake or Christmas pudding. Allow the liqueur to mature for 6 months and use for cocktails.

Chestnut cocktail Add 2 shots of chestnut liqueur to 125ml dry ginger beer, stir in some crushed ice and serve with a slice of fresh root ginger and a slice of lemon.

Elderflower vodka

SEASON	June–early July
INFUSION TIME	1–2 days

For me, nothing heralds the arrival of summer like the elderflower. Although a few of its blossoms appear in late May, it is in June that this tree comes into full flower. The sweet fragrance is entrancing, though not to everyone's liking – for some it has the distinct odour of cat's wee. The aroma of the blossoms and the long, paired leaflets make it an easy plant to identify, but it seems people do not always pay close attention and the flowers of the wayfaring tree, rowan, dogwood, hogweed and even the deadly hemlock have been mistaken for it. If the elderflower is unknown to you then do check in a guidebook. Pick the fresh, yellow-centred blossoms in full sun and use them within a few hours.

Makes about 500ml
About 30 elderflower heads
2 tsp sugar
About 500ml vodka

Remove the tiny elderflowers from the spray of blossoms using a fork (forking off, in the jargon). Loosely fill a 500ml Kilner jar with them, sprinkle on the sugar, top up with vodka and close the lid. Shake for a few minutes to dissolve the sugar.

After a day or two, strain off the infused vodka into a bottle. It is ready to drink straight away. This is not a drink to take straight, being more useful in cocktails.

Elderflower cocktail A simple, refreshing summer drink can be made by mixing elderflower vodka with another infusion: Lemon liqueur (see p.53). Put a shot of each of the infusions into your shaker, shake with crushed ice, pour into a glass and add your favourite lemonade or soda, a few leaves of wild sorrel (decidedly optional) and a slice of lemon. This is remarkably like a sweet elderflower sparkly but much quicker, easier and safer. For the real thing see p.127.

Gorse flower white rum

SEASON	Best in April, but available most of the year
INFUSION TIME	2 days

Gorse is nearly always in flower. The old saying 'When gorse is out of blossom, kissing's out of fashion' has a strong element of truth in it, but April, when every bush turns a dazzling yellow, is the best time to pick, St George's Day, 23rd April, being traditional. A warm sunny day is best.

Picking gorse flowers is even more lethal than picking blackberries or nettles. You will usually come away bloodied in some way unless you go dressed for battle, so wellington boots, leather gauntlets and a chainmail vest are essential accoutrements. It also takes a long time to pick, so bring reinforcements with you if you can.

The smell from a gorse bush in spring sunshine is very powerful and one can be overwhelmed by the aroma of the coconut-scented flowers. But it is coconut with a slight difference. Perhaps a little more like a vanilla joss stick or the vanilla-scented air freshener I put in my car once to counteract the effects of the great oyster disaster of 2009 (an entire dustbin of them overturned during an emergency stop and I only found most of them).

Makes about 500ml
A handful of gorse flowers
2 tsp sugar
About 500ml white rum (or brandy)

The moment you arrive home, loosely pack a 500ml Kilner jar with gorse flower blossoms, sprinkle on the sugar and top up with white rum. Close the lid and shake gently.

Strain the liquor into bottles after 2 days. It is ready to use immediately.

Gorse flower cocktail Gorse flower white rum retains its coconut flavour very well, but there is also an undertone of pineapple. This effectively gives you an instant Piña Colada if you add lemonade. If you like pineapples a lot, then use half lemonade, half pineapple juice for the cocktail.

Rose petal vodka

SEASON	June–August
INFUSION TIME	1 day

The summer hedgerows abound with dog rose and field rose and it is possible to make an infusion from these pretty blooms. However, their bouquet is slight and they are best left where they are. If, however, you see a startlingly pink, dense rose bush in the hedgerow it is likely to be the most useful of all the invasive plants – the Japanese rose, *Rosa rugosa*. This tough and vigorous plant is a common weed of dunes and hedgerows near to towns and even more common in the place where it is not a weed – gardens. It is remarkable for several reasons – the flowers and rosehips can often be found on the plant at the same time, the hips are simply enormous and the flowers produce the sweetest smell of all the roses. There is no need to remove the entire flower, just pull off the petals and infuse them as soon as you get home.

Makes about 500ml
About 500ml Japanese rose petals
2 tsp sugar
About 500ml vodka or eau de vie

Fairly tightly fill a 500ml Kilner jar to the brim with rose petals, sprinkle on the sugar and top up with vodka. The colour fades from the petals within hours and by the next day they will be an unappealing grey.

After a day, strain off the rose petals and bottle the liqueur. It is pinkish to start with but soon turns an attractive dark amber colour. It is ready to drink immediately. The flavour is as glorious as one would expect and the temptation to dab it behind your ears irresistible. As with most of these drinks, rose petal vodka is best used to make a cocktail (see p.63).

Pink pint

SEASON	August–September
INFUSION TIME	Not applicable

In the late 1960s I worked at the Royal Aircraft Establishment in Farnborough as a junior scientific officer. To alleviate the tedium of this bachelor existence, I would slip across the road to the pub with my drinking companions, including one by the name of Armando Cuthbert Darlington. Wearing his name with pride and a dash of fortitude, he would sit on a bar stool all evening smoking Black Russian cigarettes and drinking a potent compound called Parfait Amour. He offered me some once – it tasted like the perfume counter at Boots. This recipe is a homage to Armando.

Before we explore this – one of the most successful of all summer cocktails and my gift to the world – I need to tell you how to make rosehip syrup. This denizen of the medicine cabinet has fallen into sad disuse but is fairly easy to make and, being packed with vitamin C, is terribly good for you. It can be made from any rosehip, including the garden varieties such as *Rosa rugosa*.

Makes about 750ml syrup
For the rosehip syrup
500g rosehips
250g sugar

Serves 1
For the cocktail
150g raspberries
2 shots of rose petal vodka (see p.61)
2 shots of rosehip syrup
Lemonade

To make the rosehip syrup, put the intact rosehips into a pan and pour on enough water to just cover them. Bring to a simmer and cook until they are soft, but for at least 20 minutes. Mash the rosehips with a potato masher and squeeze the juice through a double layer of muslin. Clean the cloth and squeeze the juice through again to ensure the hairs on the seeds are removed as they are an irritant.

Return the strained juice to the cleaned pan, bring to a gentle boil and add the sugar. Stir until it is dissolved. Pour the rosehip syrup into warm, sterilised bottles. It keeps well in the fridge for at least a month.

To make the cocktail, squeeze the raspberries through a fine sieve and put them into a cocktail shaker. Add the rose petal vodka, rosehip syrup and some ice, shake and pour into a tall glass. Pour over some lemonade. It is a remarkably refreshing drink, very pink and with a pink head. A pink pint!

Dandelion brandy

SEASON	Late March–early May
INFUSION TIME	2 days

The dandelion must be the most familiar and common of all flowers in the British countryside. Although the flowers can make an appearance at any time of the year, 95% of them bloom in a flamboyant spring flush, from the end of March to the beginning of May – turning roadsides, fields, hedgerows and untended lawns golden. A single field may blossom with a million flowers – one of the least appreciated sights in the countryside. For an unassuming flower it makes a surprisingly pleasant liqueur – bittersweet with a hint of barley sugar. The colour is a pretty golden yellow.

You may have noticed that dandelions are rather variable in appearance. This is because the dandelion is really a species-complex with over two hundred micro-species in this country alone. Despite this variability it is difficult to confuse them with the many superficially similar plants such as the hawkbits – not that it would matter much if you did.

As with any flower destined for the kitchen, the dandelion should be picked in full sun and preferably in the morning. Dandelions shut up shop for the night by closing their petals and will even do this after being picked, so you will need to start your infusion the very moment you get home. At least the flowers are easy to pick and the large number of blossoms needed can be collected in just a few minutes. The petals are the least bitter part of the plants so, unless you are keen to have a bitter drink, cut the petals from the flower heads with scissors.

You will be pleased to note that I have not fallen into the temptation of calling this drink 'dandy brandy'.

Makes about 500ml
**Enough dandelion petals to fill
a 500ml Kilner jar when lightly
pressed down
2 tsp sugar
About 500ml brandy**

Put all the ingredients into a 500ml Kilner jar, seal the lid and shake until most of the sugar has dissolved.

Strain the infused brandy into bottles 2 days later. It is ready to use immediately.

Watermint vodka

SEASON	April–November
INFUSION TIME	2 days

Watermint is one of the most overlooked of wild edible plants. It grows in nearly every stream, damp path and watermeadow and can be picked with abandon. The slightly hairy, dark green to purple leaves are easily spotted and when in pink-purple flower the plant is unmistakable. It also smells strongly of peppermint. The stem is tough and wiry so you need to cut it with scissors to avoid uprooting the whole thing.

Vodka takes up the minty flavour very quickly and you will have your watermint vodka perfectly drinkable in 4 hours or so. If you include sugar with the leaves – or even add it later – you will effectively have something similar to crème de menthe. The major difference is that the latter is made from the tiny leaves of the potent Corsican mint, *Mentha requienii*, which is sometimes found here growing in gardens.

Watermint vodka takes some drinking on its own unless you like mint flavours a lot. Like its commercial brother it is best used in cocktails such as Grasshopper (equal quantities of crème de menthe or watermint vodka, crème de cacao and fresh cream), though whether this really improves things is entirely a matter of opinion.

Perhaps watermint vodka's greatest use is as an after-dinner liqueur or a 'hair of the dog' hangover cure. Mint contains a couple of ingredients which settle the stomach. There also seems to be some truth to the notion that an alcoholic drink the next day will restore some much needed equilibrium. The brain, having had its activity depressed by alcohol, fights back by over-stimulating it. A morning-after drink will depress it back to something resembling normal.

You may also come across the long serrated leaves of wild spearmint, *M. spicata*, in the hedgerow. This can be used instead if you like your drink to taste of toothpaste.

Makes about 250ml

**About 20 watermint leaves, plus
a sprig with flowers on if possible,
or 1 tbsp Corsican mint leaves**

**1 tbsp sugar
About 250ml vodka**

Put the watermint (or mint) leaves, sugar and vodka into a 250ml Kilner jar and shake gently. Close the lid and leave to infuse for a couple of days.

Strain the infused vodka into a bottle containing the sprig of watermint with flowers. It is ready to drink straight away.

Sweet vernal grass vodka

SEASON	May–June
INFUSION TIME	1 week

There is a remarkable Polish speciality called Żubrówka, also known as bison grass vodka. Bison grass (*Hierochloe odorata*), or holy grass as it is also known, is a bit thin on the ground in Britain, being confined to a few Scottish islands and parts of the Lake District, but we have something which is just as good – sweet vernal grass. This is the stuff that gives hay its aroma and vodka captures it perfectly and permanently.

Sweet vernal grass is fairly easy to spot with its relatively narrow and dark flower heads and distinctive smell when rubbed. Another clue is the fine hairs which appear where the tiny leaves join the stem. Pick in May or June when in flower. Żubrówka is traditionally bottled with a blade or two of the grass; I do the same but I got carried away with the one in the picture and left all the blades in. Looks good though.

An alternative is to use creamy blooms of meadowsweet, which adorn roadsides and damp meadows from the Channel Islands to the Isle of Skye. They appear in summer and linger until November. Their intense, slightly antiseptic smell can be overpowering close up and despite the best efforts of foragers they have found but small use in the kitchen except in the making of drinks, meadowsweet sparkling wine (made to the same recipe as sparkling elderflower, see p.127) being one.

Both sweet vernal grass and meadowsweet contain the highly aromatic and (slightly) toxic chemical coumarin. The tiny quantities involved are harmless – more harmless than the vodka certainly – and it is chiefly this that gives us the flavour.

Makes about 500ml

A handful of sweet vernal grass (or meadowsweet blooms)

Sugar, to taste (optional)
About 500ml vodka (a good one)

Cut the grass to length to fit into a 500ml Kilner jar (or loosely pack meadowsweet flowers). Top up with vodka and close the lid. Store in a dark cupboard, shaking once a day. This takes a week to infuse properly (meadowsweet needs only a day). Add a little sugar to sweeten if you like. Strain and bottle. It is ready immediately.

Szarlotka For this cocktail my friend Monika who hails from Poland and knows all about Żubrówka suggests: 2 shots of the infused vodka mixed with 4 shots of fresh apple juice and crushed ice. *Szarlotka*, Monika tells me, is Polish for apple pie. *Na zdrowie*!

Fennel vodka

SEASON	May–June
INFUSION TIME	2 weeks

Fennel is a common garden plant but also frequently found at roadsides and, for reasons best known to itself, around seaside car parks. The leaves, available throughout much of the year, the bright yellow flowers of summer, and the seeds, found in summer and autumn, can all be used for this infusion. It is one to which I never add sugar. Fennel itself is sweet, not from sugar, but from anethole, the chemical which provides the typical anise flavour and which is many times sweeter than sucrose.

An easy variation is to use sweet cicely, another member of the Apiaceae (carrot family). Outside of the garden this is a plant of northern climes, seldom making an appearance below Birmingham to the west or York to the east. In its northern fastness it can take the place of the considerably less delicious cow parsley, which fills the roadsides of the south. As its name suggests, it too is sweet; the immature seed pods particularly so and these can be eaten straight from the plant as sweetmeats.

Whichever plant, or part of the plant, you use you will have a drink not dissimilar to Pernod, pastis and ouzo, all of which derive from anise – yet another member of the Apiaceae, but one not found in Britain.

Makes about 250ml
1 tsp fennel or sweet cicely seeds
A sprig or two of the leaves of fennel
  or sweet cicely or the flower heads
About 250ml vodka

Put all the ingredients into a 250ml Kilner jar, close the lid and shake gently. Store in a dark cupboard, shaking gently once a day.

Decant the infused vodka into a bottle after 2 weeks and pop in a couple of the fennel (or sweet cicely) leaves or flower heads for artistic purposes. It is also possible to use just the leaves or both leaves and seeds. The drink is ready to use immediately.

Absinthe

SEASON	November–April (for Alexanders)
INFUSION TIME	4 weeks

In the early twentieth century a particularly notorious drink was banned throughout most of the Western world. It is called absinthe. This is an anise-flavoured drink but the ingredient that caused so much heart searching and disagreement is another herb – wormwood. The manufacturing process is part-infusion, part-distillation, with the various herbaceous ingredients steeped in warm water for 12 hours, strong alcohol added and the resultant liquor distilled. The colour, itself taken from various plants, is a later addition.

The big question, of course, is this: Does absinthe deserve its notoriety? Many at the time were in no doubt, the *Pall Mall Gazette* of 1868 among them:

If a visitor to Paris strolls along the Boulevards from the Madeleine to the Bastille some summer's afternoon, between five and six o'clock, which is commonly called the 'hour of the absinthe', he can hardly fail to remark hundreds of Parisians seated outside the various cafés, or lounging at the counters of the wine shops, and imbibing this insidious stimulant… It is an ignoble poison, destroying life not until it has more or less brutalised its votaries, and made drivelling idiots of them.

The ills ascribed to absinthe – hallucinations, tendency to criminal activity, death and so on – were blamed on a chemical called thujone, which is derived from one of its principal ingredients, wormwood. Thujone is known to be toxic in sufficiently large doses, but absinthe, it has recently been discovered from bottles surviving from the time, contained only small amounts. Much more likely it was straightforward alcohol poisoning. *The Lancet* of the time tells us:

At any rate, it will take a good deal of very solid and precise evidence to convince us that the trifling amount of essence of wormwood contained in the liquor called absinthe, adds any considerable poisonous power to the natural influence of some 20 or 30 ounces per diem of a highly concentrated alcohol, which is what many of these Parisian buveurs actually dispose of in the course of innumerable visits to the cafés and other houses of refreshment.

Thirty ounces is about 1½ pints and absinthe was anything from 48–88% ABV so it is little surprise that things went awry. Today absinthe has been exonerated and rehabilitated as a legal drink, because very little thujone survives the brewing process, though hitting the juice like Toulouse-Lautrec and his peers will still have you singing 'La Carmagnole' and storming the Bastille.

So it is that I feel justified in offering my own recipe. For reasons of legality we cannot follow the traditional distillation process but will use instead the method employed for making cheap absinthe – an infusion. A treatise on the Manufacture and Distillation of Alcoholic Liquors of 1871 gives several intriguing recipes using a variety of ingredients which are readily available. It is the absinthe maker's bible and I highly recommend it to those who wish to experiment further.

Wormwood (*Artemisia absinthium*) is an occasional plant found typically on the coast of the British Isles but also in scattered locations elsewhere, particularly the Midlands. It is an extraordinary plant with an extraordinary smell, and it is not one I would like to take through customs. With this, safety and the relative rarity of the plant in mind only a tiny amount is used, so just snip off a few leaves. The amount of wormwood I suggest below is perfectly safe unless you have epilepsy (and I would not like to see expectant or nursing mothers knocking back absinthe either).

Absinthe is famously green, hence its name 'The Green Fairy', and if you would like yours to be green too then you can use the traditional plant for colouring. Find some brooklime – it grows in streams and along damp paths – crush the leaves with a pestle and mortar and add at the beginning with the other ingredients.

If you wish to experiment then try adding Alexanders seeds or hogweed seeds with everything else. These are wild analogues of other plants often used in the manufacture of absinthe.

Makes about 500ml

4g dried wormwood leaves (optional)
30g green aniseed or star anise
20g fresh fennel leaves
20g leaves and stems of Alexanders
   (see p.76) or angelica

20g brooklime leaves, crushed
   (optional)
50g sugar
400–500ml vodka

Place the dried wormwood leaves, if using, aniseed, fresh fennel leaves, Alexanders, brooklime, if using, and sugar in a 500ml Kilner jar and cover with the vodka. Close the lid and leave for 4 weeks to allow the flavours to pass to the alcohol.

Strain off the seeds and leaves, and bottle the infused liquor. Leave to mature for 3 months before drinking or knock it back straight away if you can't wait.

Absinthe is traditionally sipped from an absinthe glass. A special absinthe spoon is placed over the glass, a rectangular cube (yes, I know) of sugar is placed on the spoon and water slowly dripped on to it until the correct level of sweetness is achieved. Evidently Parisians had special dispensers – absinthe fountains – which would drip water for you; no doubt it saved time for those determined to get through their daily pint.

Gin Alexanders

SEASON	November–April
INFUSION TIME	2 weeks

There is a well-known cocktail called Gin Alexanders but this is the real thing – gin *and* Alexanders. Alexanders is a very common roadside plant found around the more southerly coasts of Britain. It is an easy plant to identify: the leaves are relatively large, yellow-green and shallowly lobed, and the aromatic smell is unmistakable – just like angelica (if you know what that smells like). It is very important to get this right as in the spring a rather similar plant in the same family, hemlock waterdropwort, can be found in damp places and very often by the sea. It has smaller, darker leaves, which are incised not lobed, and has an intense and unpleasant smell. It is one of the most deadly plants on the planet.

An odd characteristic of Alexanders is that in early winter, when everything else is settling down for a rest, it starts to produce its succulent leaves and shoots. I pick it from early November until April, when the stems toughen to the texture of bamboo.

Alexanders is sometimes steamed and served with butter or candied to make an unusual sweetmeat, but in whatever form it comes, it is rather an acquired taste and pretty well indescribable to the uninitiated. However, I do think Gin Alexanders shows the plant at its best as the flavours of the two ingredients are rather similar.

Makes about 500ml
About 6 Alexanders stems (30cm long)
**   and leaves**
About 500ml gin
1 tbsp sugar

Chop up the Alexanders stems, put them in a 750ml Kilner jar with the leaves and pour on the gin. Leave to infuse for a couple of weeks, then decant into a bottle and add the sugar. It is ready to drink straight away.

Quick method To speed things up, crush the stems then squeeze out the juice through muslin straight into the gin, adding the sugar.

To drink The bitter taste of Gin Alexanders taken straight is perhaps a little too invigorating for most palates but it works nicely with a good lemonade and crushed ice, served with a stem of Alexanders for decoration if you have one to hand.

Rhubarb vodka

SEASON	March–July
INFUSION TIME	3 months

I do not entirely approve of gardening, but I am willing to grow a few maintenance-free plants like herbs, apple trees and, most important of all, rhubarb. I planted my rhubarb in a sheltered corner next to the shed and within a year it had grown to about five feet across and looked like it had been there since the Coronation. It is an exciting time when the first sticks appear and these are the best ones to use in an infusion, though it is perfectly good up until midsummer.

Rhubarb vodka is the best 'fruit' infusion of them all and I have had to hide my stash in a distant cupboard as guests have taken to helping themselves once they have had a taste. With most infusions I suggest making a little first before tackling a big batch but go straight for a half-gallon of rhubarb vodka – you won't be disappointed.

A first-class variation on the recipe is to add ginger – a few slices of root ginger will work their wonders. Another is to add sweet cicely pods or leaves. The leaves of sweet cicely are available from spring until the late summer and the pods from late June to early July.

Makes about 600ml
280g rhubarb stalks
150g sugar
About 600ml vodka

Optional flavourings
A couple of slices of ginger *or*
2 tsp sweet cicely pods/a couple of sweet cicely leaves

Slice the rhubarb into 3–6mm lengths (a mandolin is ideal for this, if a bit scary) and layer in a 1-litre Kilner jar alternately with the sugar and flavouring (if you have opted for one). Pour over the vodka and close the lid. Leave for a couple of days, then shake the jar once a day until all the sugar has dissolved.

Decant the vodka into bottles after 3 months. It is ready straight away.

Quick method To speed things up, sprinkle the sugar on to the rhubarb first and give it a shake every day for 4 days to extract the juice by osmosis. Then add the vodka, shake and wait until all the sugar has dissolved. Strain out the rhubarb and bottle the liqueur. Incidentally, the slightly alcoholic rhubarb is softened and sweetened by this process and quite unbelievably delicious with ice cream.

Green walnut grappa

SEASON	June–July
INFUSION TIME	6 weeks

A long time ago I spent a couple of weeks in Italy with an Italian lady friend, visiting her rather large extended family. Her aunt Maria lived in a farmhouse somewhere between Rome and Naples. It had *no* sanitation and the electrical supply consisted of cables draped like Christmas decorations around the house, but it was one of the happiest homes I have ever visited. We sat outside, raised an arm to pick figs, played bocce, ate the best home cooking in the world and drank – mostly good wine.

It was forty years ago but I can still recall the taste of Aunt Maria's grappa infusion. It was an opaque pale green colour and sufficiently thick to stand a spoon upright in it. The flavour was cloyingly sweet and seemingly arrived at by infusing everything from the shelves of a well-stocked herbalist, with unripe walnuts in the mix. It was too much for me, though I did manage to down a glass of the noxious stuff.

To be fair, most herbal liqueurs are made to promote good health, not to provide entertainment and auntie's drink was probably designed as a *digestivo*. I am afraid that Aunt Maria is no longer with us so I rely on a recipe sent by my friend Monica.

Makes about 1 litre

10 large green walnuts, or 15 small ones (soft enough for a fork to penetrate the young shell inside)
About 1 litre grappa (or brandy)
250–400g sugar, depending on how sweet you like your drinks

Flavourings
2 roasted dandelion roots (3 coffee beans will do) *or*
2 tsp hogweed or Alexander seeds (a few cloves, a cinnamon stick and ½ mace blade will do)

Wear gloves before handling the nuts – extract of walnut husks are used to this day as an excellent wood stain, one that takes a couple of weeks to wash off the hands. Slice the green walnuts into quarters, then again to give you about 8 pieces from each – it does not have to be exact. Put them in a 1.5-litre Kilner jar with your chosen flavouring ingredients, then top up with grappa. Leave the jar on a sunny windowsill for 6 weeks.

Strain the grappa into another jar. Gently heat the sugar in a little hot water until dissolved and add this to the strained liquor. Bottle and leave for another 6 weeks before drinking.

Épine apéritif

SEASON	May–August
INFUSION TIME	2 weeks

The leaves of some trees are considered to be edible by a few wild-food enthusiasts though I have always had my doubts. As an inveterate hedgerow nibbler I have tried most of those that won't actually poison me and found little to inspire. Apart from Beech Leaf Noyau (see Pam Corbin's recipe in the *River Cottage Preserves Handbook*) I had never tried a tree-leaf infusion until recently when I was delighted to receive a bottle of homemade épine apéritif from my friend Sarah, who discovered the drink during a long sojourn in France. It is different from other infusions in that it also contains wine (lots of it). Fortunately Sarah gave me the recipe too.

Blackthorn, that prickly denizen of hedgerows from Penzance to Peterhead, is of course famous for the making of sloe gin, yet it came as a surprise to me to learn that blackthorn leaves make a drink which is every bit as good. The blackthorn leaves give the drink the almond flavour that you find in sloe gin, while the wine provides the acid. The finished drink is an extraordinary treat – fruity, rich and very strong.

A small word of warning is appropriate here. While the leaves of blackthorn are harmless, the same cannot be said for some other members of Prunus such as the bird cherry. These contain fairly high levels of cyanic compounds which have been known to cause problems (death). Stick to blackthorn and everything will be fine.

The blackthorn leaves are best picked fairly young from mid-April to midsummer. In France they use red wine but a blackberry or elderberry wine is more appropriate for us home brewers.

Makes about 2.85 litres

About 500ml blackthorn leaves
2.5 litres red wine, or homemade red fruit wine such as blackberry or elderberry

350ml brandy or eau de vie
500g sugar

Put all the ingredients into a small plastic fermenting bucket (see the wine section, p.101, for more on these). Stir until the sugar has dissolved, then fit the lid tightly. Leave for 2 weeks, stirring occasionally.

Strain through a funnel lined with a double layer of muslin into clean bottles. Leave to mature for a year or so. *Santé*!

Oak moss gin

SEASON	All year
INFUSION TIME	1 month

This is one of the oddest things in a book full of odd things. Despite a lifetime of eating wild mushrooms I had never tried lichen until very recently. Lichens are not, generally speaking, edible, but a friend suggested I try deep-fried oak moss (*Evernia prunastri*). This common lichen is most often found on the dead twigs of oak trees, though it grows on other trees as well and one can find as much attached to fallen twigs on the ground as on the tree. Several species look a little like it and the best tip I can give you is that the undersides of the lobes are almost white, not pale green as in other species.

Oak moss is used in perfumery and as soon as you cook it you can understand why. The kitchen, and indeed the rest of the house, is filled with a pleasant aroma not dissimilar to that of an upmarket department store. The flavour simply follows the aroma.

Naturally I wondered what sort of infusion it would make so I popped some in a jam jar and poured in some gin. After 2 days all I could taste was earth and gin but it settled down after a month and the aromatic qualities came remarkably to the fore, filling the mouth with a fresh, pleasant and rather persistent perfume.

A word of warning. Although I have been unable to find any indication that oak moss is poisonous if ingested, it is known to cause an allergic skin reaction in some people. This is really a conversation-piece kind of a drink so, to err on the side of safety, I suggest drinking no more than half a shot… and don't rub it on your chest.

Makes about 250ml
½ teacupful of oak moss
About 250ml gin

Place the oak moss in a 250ml Kilner jar and pour on the gin. Close the lid and leave for a month, then strain into a bottle. It is ready immediately.

The oldest drink in the world

SEASON	All year
INFUSION TIME	3–4 months

In the summer of 2012 I was invited to take a seashore foray on the Danish island of Samsø. At the northern tip of the island I met the warden of a nature reserve, Bjorn, who showed me around the place. We then spent a good couple of hours sampling the contents of his very peculiar drinks cupboard. He was, it transpired, a brother infuser.

My sometimes odd combinations and ingredients paled in comparison to his outlandishly adventurous concoctions. Towards the end of our time in his aromatic shed he pulled from the back of the cupboard a bottle of what he called the oldest drink in the world. It seemed to have a vodka base and the flavour was reminiscent of pine trees. My guess that it was pine needle vodka was not so far away from the truth, but the ingredient which gave the drink its flavour was not a year or two old but 35 million years old. It was amber.

Anxious to try it myself, I discovered that small packets of amber are available online for next to nothing so I ordered a few grams. The result is a pleasant pine-scented liquor, although not one you would wish to knock back by the bottle. However, its great virtue is that it is such an impressive thing to offer friends.

Makes about 250ml
1 tsp amber
250ml vodka

Wash the amber, dry it, then wrap it in cling film. Lay it on a small sheet of plastic on your concrete patio and proceed to reduce it to powder with a large hammer. Place the powder in a 250ml Kilner jar and pour in the vodka. It can take several months for the flavour to develop but warming the jar in a hot water-bath will produce an instant effect. Either way the amber never seems to dissolve completely so pass the liquor through a filter paper when bottling.

A hangover cure

SEASON	All year
INFUSION TIME	2 weeks

I almost never suffer from a hangover but on the odd occasion when I have a touch too much of an evening I rather dread the terrible feeling that I know I will face in the morning. My favoured 'cure' is a pre-emptive attack on the hangover consisting of two ibuprofen tablets washed down with a pint of cocoa. This must be followed by staying awake and consuming nothing else for an hour. The regime is pretty foolproof provided you are in a fit state to *a.* make a pint of cocoa, *b.* drink a pint of cocoa, *c.* keep a pint of cocoa down and *d.* stay awake for an hour. If you can manage these things it works extremely well.

If you prefer the herbal route, my friend Monica Wilde from Napiers Herbalists in Edinburgh has supplied a recipe, which, she tells me, will make life worth living again. I asked her how this stuff worked and was informed that willow bark contained aspirin, milk thistle is for the liver, yellow gentian is bitter and gets the gastric juices flowing, mint settles the stomach and dandelion is a diuretic, stimulating your much put-upon kidneys. However, I suspect that its true *modus operandi* is to take your mind off your hangover with its flavour – it is technically called a 'herbal bitter' and it really isn't kidding. You will probably have to buy some of the flavouring ingredients, though a few are forageable.

Makes about 450ml

25g cut dried white willow bark
(*Salix alba*)
25g lightly crushed milk thistle seeds
(*Silybum marianum*)
10g chopped dried yellow gentian root
(*Gentiana lutea*)

20g dried peppermint leaves (*Mentha piperita*) but watermint (*M. aqua*), found near streams, will do nicely
20g chopped dried dandelion root
(*Taraxacum officinalis*)
About 450ml vodka

You can, if you like, just simmer all the flavouring ingredients in 1 litre water for 15 minutes, then strain off the liquid – a cupful being sufficient to brighten the day. However, much more to my liking – as it has the added benefit that comes from the 'hair of the dog' – is to prepare for the dark day beforehand: put the flavouring ingredients into a 500ml Kilner jar, top up with vodka and leave to infuse for a fortnight. Strain and bottle. Just 5ml in a little water taken every hour for up to six doses is what Monica recommends.

Wine

Wine-making was where I started my home-

brewing career and it has been a thrilling ride with a few notable derailments on the way. The wines I have included in this chapter are mostly the stalwarts of home wine-making – elderberry, elderflower, blackberry, dandelion and so on; stick with these if you want to tread a safe path. A few are a little more unusual and some can only be described as 'interesting'. As with all home brewing the best thing is to make a range of different brews then stick to the ones you like.

There is a serious bias here in favour of ingredients that you can forage – because I like them, because they make the best wines, because they are traditional and because they are free. Foraged ingredients are very much in the spirit of homemade wines; it makes them seem all the more homemade, but in a very good way.

Some flavour ingredients such as soft fruits provide a proportion of the sugar and water necessary for making wine, but many of them (floral flavourings in particular) provide neither. Wines made from these ingredients lack the fruitiness that we would usually expect. This is a combination of acidic flavours and tannins and in order to create them we often include grapes in the form of juice or raisins, or we simply add shop-bought fruit acids and tannin.

Despite a sweet tooth (the singular being increasingly appropriate), generally speaking, I prefer dry wines and most of the recipes that follow will produce a dry wine if left to follow their natural inclinations. However, if you like sweeter wines, it is easy to sweeten a dry wine before it is bottled. Alternatively, you can sweeten a wine immediately prior to serving, though, for some reason I cannot fathom, this is something we feel uncomfortable about.

The distinction between wine and beer is actually a vague one. In his survey of ancient brews, Stephen Buhner says that historically there really isn't any difference between them; in many cultures the same word or words are used indiscriminately to refer to either or both. Today things have settled down and we think of beer as coming from grains and wines coming from grapes. Country wines are made from anything that is not a grape and to which sugar is added. Sadly they are considered to be poor relations of their noble cousins, and certainly it is a very good country wine that can surpass a first-class grape wine. However comparisons are futile; they are different things. Certainly, you should never be ashamed of your home-brewed creations, not without good reason at least.

The method

Wine-making is fairly straightforward, with a few variations. Generally, water and sugar are added to one or more flavour ingredients, then the fluid is separated from the solid matter (or not), and the resulting liquid is fermented. There is no single method, there are several, but this is an outline of how wine can be made at home. The recipe for Rhubarb wine (on p.108) is a model for most of those that follow.

Preparing the main ingredients Fruit (and vegetables) need to be washed thoroughly and finely sliced, chopped or squashed and placed in a fermenting bucket. There is no point in washing flowers or herbs.

Adding sugar Sugar is stirred in and left to absorb the juices and flavours.

Adding water Hot water is poured over the fruit/vegetable/flower and sugar mix and left to cool to room temperature (about 18°C). A crushed Campden tablet *can* be added at this point (see p.98). Please note that sometimes the sugar and water are added at the same time and that sometimes the water used is cold.

Additional ingredients Other ingredients such as pectic enzyme, yeast nutrient, tannin, fruit acids, grape concentrate, lemon juice, etc. are stirred in. The totality of mixture prior to and during fermentation is called the must (from *mustum*, the Latin for 'new wine').

Adjusting specific gravity The specific gravity of the must (which indicates the sugar concentration) is measured and adjusted upwards with sugar or, rarely, downwards with cold water.

Aeration The must is aerated with a whisk or something similar.

Pitching Yeast is added ('pitched') and a prayer offered.

Primary fermentation The must is stirred once a day until fermentation has slowed – about 5 or 6 days. During the primary fermentation a large number of yeast cells are produced in the presence of oxygen (aerobic conditions).

Transferring to a second fermenter The must is left for a day without stirring then siphoned or strained into a demi-john or other container (pic 1), leaving the lees (dead yeast at the bottom of the bucket) and other solid matter behind. An air lock is fitted to the demi-john (pic 2).

Siphoning the must from the fermenting bucket into a demi-john

Fitting an air lock to the demi-john

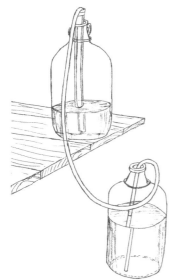

Racking the wine into a clean demi-john after the second fermentation

Siphoning the wine into bottles

Secondary fermentation The demi-john is kept at room temperature until the fermentation has ceased or almost ceased. This second stage of fermentation, when the yeast lives without oxygen (anaerobically) and produces alcohol, is a much more sedate affair than the first. It can take anything from 3 weeks to 2 months depending on a number of factors, particularly temperature. When air bubbles are no longer emitting from the air lock (or slow to one every few minutes), this stage is complete.

Racking and fining The contents of the demi-john are siphoned into a fresh demi-john (pic 3, p.91), leaving the lees behind, and again an air lock is fitted. Wine finings are often added to clear the wine. To ensure anaerobic fermentation the demi-john must be full. Any shortfall is made up with a sugar solution (made with 3 parts boiled water to 1 part sugar and cooled), or some sterilised glass marbles.

Clearing The must is left until all signs of fermentation have ceased and what now may be called wine is clear. This will take at least a couple of months.

Sweetening and bottling If you want a dry wine, or you have used sufficient sugar to ensure a sweet one, then your wine is ready to bottle (pic 4, p.91). For advice on bottling, see pp.102–3. If you want a sweet wine and the wine is dry (intentionally or not), follow the sterilisation and sweetening process described on p.95.

Making a dry wine

Provided there is not too much for it to cope with, yeast will consume all the fermentable sugar in a must. For this reason it is easy to produce a wine that is dry; you just use a limited amount of sugar and dry it will be. Of course it is the amount of sugar that ends up in the must that matters, not necessarily the amount you add. Some ingredients, such as blackberries, add sugar to a must and others, like rhubarb, actually take some away. Therefore before you start a fermentation you should test the must for sugar level with a hydrometer and, if necessary, adjust it upwards by stirring in sugar syrup or caster sugar or, more rarely, downward by adding water.

The specific gravity before fermentation starts is called the original gravity (OG), see p.14. To make a dry wine, the original gravity should be in the range 1085–1105. The low part of the range will be very dry indeed and the high part slightly sweet – though such things as the activity of the yeast and temperature can affect sweetness too. For most of the wines in this book I take a middle path and suggest an original gravity of 1095. This will give you a dry wine, but it is open to you to go for anything in that range if you want. Knowing the original gravity of what will be a dry wine also gives a fairly accurate indication of its alcohol content.

Making a sweet wine

Most of the recipes in this chapter will make a dry wine unless you either add more sugar right from the start or at the end after it has been stabilised. To add sugar from the start, one can simply use 'too much' sugar in the must before fermentation; the yeast then consumes all it can manage and some sugar is left over at the end as a sweetener.

This is a time-honoured method of making a sweet or medium sweet wine, and it is the way that many wines are made at home. It is a little hit and miss as it is never possible to determine exactly how sweet your wine will be – sickly sweet wines are seldom to anyone's taste and I consider them to be the bane of home wine-making. While only a few of the recipes that follow suggest this method, there is always the option of adding more sugar to the original must of a dry wine should you wish.

The following table gives the original gravity (OG) you will need for sweet and medium sweet wine – and also for dry. It also provides the likely final gravity (FG), which is the specific gravity of the finished wine; the higher the final gravity the sweeter the wine.

STYLE	ORIGINAL GRAVITY (OG)	FINAL GRAVITY (FG)
Sweet	1120–30	1005–15
Medium	1105–20	995–1005
Dry	1085–1105	990–1000

It is useful to know that every 100g sugar added to 5 litres of must will increase the specific gravity by 7.5 points. So, for example, 200g added to a must at 1090 will result in a must at 1105.

Sweetening a dry wine

The most precise approach for making sweet wine, and the default method used in most of the recipes here, is to make a dry wine and then sweeten it. The problem with this is that any yeast cells remaining in the brew may be delighted to be presented with more food and carry on devouring sugar where they left off, consuming all or most of it. It is therefore necessary to kill the yeast cells.

In commercial wines this is done by filtering out the yeast using industrial-grade filters under pressure. As far as I know, there are no domestic versions of these machines so we must employ chemical methods. Here is the process in brief.

A dry wine is made as usual, but instead of bottling it straight away, a tiny amount of potassium sorbate is added. Potassium sorbate is an organic salt of sorbic acid – a fruit acid found in rowan and other berries. It has the peculiar ability to prevent reproduction in yeast cells: birth control for yeast. There will be no more yeast babies and the yeasts will eventually die out. However, there will still be some yeast cells left so these are killed with sodium metabisulphite. The wine has now been 'stabilised'.

If you are feeling alarmed at this point I quite understand but rest assured – both these chemicals are harmless in the minute quantities used. The 'acceptable daily intake' of potassium sorbate is about 2g for the average person. This would require the consumption of two gallons of wine in a single day, a drinking session that would likely make you flammable and certainly dead. The sulphur dioxide that derives from sodium metabisulphite is even more forgiving and mostly dissipates anyway.

Sugar is then added until the required degree of sweetness has been reached and the wine is bottled as normal.

Method for sweetening wine with sugar syrup Follow the directions for making a dry wine, but do not bottle it once it has been racked into the second demi-john. Instead, allow the wine to ferment out and clear completely.

Rack into a third demi-john and add ½ tsp potassium sorbate (1g) dissolved in a little boiled, warm water. Do not exceed this amount. Close the demi-john and leave for 24 hours. Now add one crushed Campden tablet, again dissolved in a little water. Close the demi-john and leave for a further 24 hours.

Make up a sugar syrup by dissolving 100g sugar in 150ml water over a medium heat and bringing to the boil. Remove about 150ml wine from the demi-john, keeping it in a covered sterilised container. Add some of the sugar syrup to the wine in the demi-john and, making sure it is evenly distributed (not easy!), test it for sweetness. Add more if necessary and test again. Fill any remaining space in the demi-john with the previously extracted wine. Bottle.

It is worth mentioning two other methods of sweetening wine:

Sweetening with sugar Adding sugar immediately prior to serving is the easiest way to sweeten a wine. People baulk at this but it is a method with a venerable and honourable history.

Sweetening with lactose Alternatively you can add lactose syrup to the wine just prior to bottling. This sugar is unfermentable so there will be no problems with it being lost to the yeast and no disasters from corks popping or bottles exploding from the carbon dioxide produced during re-fermentation. However, do remember that some people cannot tolerate lactose.

The ingredients

The primary ingredients will be those you wish to name on the label – blackberry, rosehip, and so on. There seems to be no limit to what can be turned into a wine, which, as I have indicated, can be a problem. Very few things will not make a passable wine provided the sweetness, tartness, alcohol level and so on are managed successfully, but to make a really good wine you need outstanding ingredients. They should have a strong and pleasant flavour or aroma. Fruits make the best wine in my opinion because they provide their own acids and sometimes tannin, but with the addition of fruit acids, the floral wines can have a lightness and fragrance typical of some first-class white wines.

Sugar

Cheap granulated sugar is fine for nearly all the recipes here, though if you want to spend the money then the organic, slightly brown stuff will be fine. More complex (and expensive) sugars such as molasses, coconut sugar, agave sugar and so on are far too strongly flavoured for wines and some of these exotic sugars can also contain unfermentable sugars which will impart an unavoidable extra and possibly unwanted sweetness. Honey, of course, is a time-honoured source of sugar and it is included in some of the recipes.

Grape juice

This is the part where we seem to be cheating as grape juice adds 'vinosity' to wine, that is, it makes your wine taste like wine. Grape juice, in the form of concentrates, adds body, tannin and fruitiness (acidity) to many wines and without it they can taste a little 'thin'. Although you can add acids and tannins to your must, the benefits can be achieved by using grape concentrate. It is available in red and white, with a single 250ml tin being sufficient for one demi-john of wine. The tinned concentrates are made from wine grape varieties.

You can use cheap grape juice but this is made from dessert grapes and is fairly sweet and without much acidity; also you may need to rest the must for 24 hours if the juice contains sulphur dioxide preservative (labelled as E220); and if it contains potassium sorbate (E202) or similar you will get nowhere at all as this prevents yeasts from breeding.

The traditional alternative to grape concentrate or juice is raisins; these are coarsely chopped and added to the must. They are less used now, partly because they tend to make all your wines taste like bread pudding. Sometimes this is not a bad thing and I have used raisins in the ginger wine recipe and elsewhere.

Both raisins and grape concentrate contain about half their weight in sugar and this has been allowed for in the recipes.

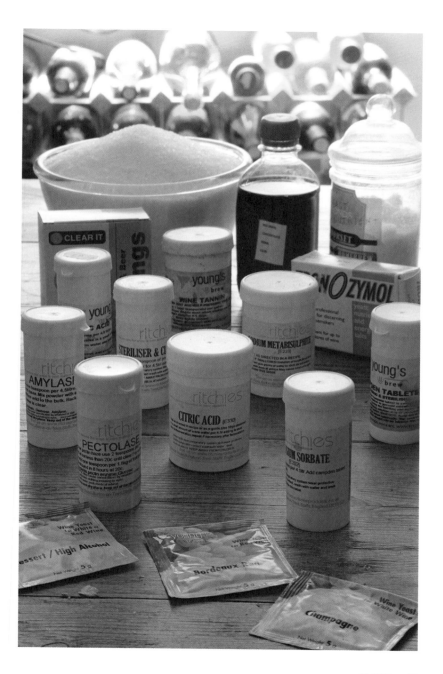

Acids

Although most fruit wines are acidic enough to not require the addition of acidic ingredients, floral and vegetable wines need an acid boost. Low acidity in wine will not merely give you a bland wine, it can also result in slow yeast growth and the development of unwanted micro-organisms. The acidity level required is quite 'high', with a pH of between 3.2 and 3.6 (the lower the pH the higher the acidity). Knowing the required pH value is pretty useless if you do not possess a pH meter, though narrow-range acidity-testing strips are available very cheaply.

To boost acidity the fruit acids – malic, citric and tartaric – are often employed. These are readily available as crystals in little pots and you can buy all three in a mix under the name of 'acid blend'. Alternatively you can add them by employing acidic fruits such as lemon, lime, crab apple and sea buckthorn.

Tannin

This bitter-tasting substance is found in abundance in grapes and apples, especially crab apples. Without tannins a wine tastes as though it has something seriously missing, so tannin, in one form or another, is often added. Grape concentrates provide tannin and it is possible to buy grape tannin as a powder. At one time teabags were used to introduce tannin into a wine – I stick to the powder.

Pectic enzyme

As a dedicated maker of jam I have always appreciated the gelling properties of pectin, which make jam set. For the wine maker it is nothing but a nuisance. Many fruits contain the protein pectin, which makes itself evident as an annoying, if harmless, 'pectin haze' sometimes seen in wines. Fortunately it is easy to avoid provided you take action at the beginning of the process and do not try to fix things later. (As a guide, if a fruit makes jam easily it contains a great deal of pectin.) Pectin is easily removed by pectic enzyme, which should be added to the must at least 8 hours before the yeast is pitched because it is deactivated in the presence of alcohol. It is available in crystalline form under various names, such as pectolase.

Amylase

This enzyme is of fundamental importance in the production of beer but only needed occasionally in wine-making. Starchy ingredients like parsnips and bananas can haze a wine with fine particles of starch. These can be avoided by adding a small quantity of amylase (1 level tsp per 4.5 litres) to the must before the yeast is pitched.

Campden tablets

Adding a crushed Campden tablet to the must as a matter of course is, strictly speaking, optional. The point of adding one is that it will kill any (or at least most) unwanted yeast and any spoilage bacteria. Generally, I do not use them as the yeast that is added at the next stage will be a vigorous, modern variety which usually out-performs any interlopers; and the boiling water, if used, is normally sufficient to sterilise the must anyway. If, however, I'm not convinced that all extraneous bugs will be dead before fermentation begins then I always employ them; if you want to be assured that nothing unpleasant gets into your brew then feel free to use one.

If you do, then leave the tablet to do its work for 24 hours before you move on to the next stage. By that time the sulphur dioxide will have dissipated or turned into a minute quantity of sulphuric acid.

Plums have always been a problem for me as they seem to come ready-loaded with any amount of biological baggage, so for plum wine and one or two other fruit wines I either use a Campden tablet or heat-treat the must by bringing it nearly to the boil.

Yeast nutrient

Many musts contain a sufficiency of other nutrients for the yeast, but many do not. For these a proprietary yeast nutrient should be stirred into the must before the yeast is pitched. For the most part you will get away with common yeast nutrients which provide just nitrogen, but some very low-nutrient brews, such as rice wine, require something containing more varied fare.

Yeast

As someone who is very easily distracted, I once found a fermenting bucket behind the sofa containing the must of a fruit wine that I had started 5 days previously and forgotten about. It was bubbling away vigorously even though I had added no yeast. There is always enough yeast floating around in the air or stuck to fruit skins to start a fermentation without the need to add any from a packet. Unfortunately it can take time to get going and you have no idea which of several score of wild yeast species and strains you will end up with. I was lucky on that occasion – indeed most of the time only *Saccharomyces cerevisiae* of one sort or another survives the brewing process – but it is not a good general policy – better to add something with a label on it.

Yeasts do not just produce alcohol. They also create the esters that give wine much of its flavour – imagine adding vodka to grape juice and you will see what I mean. The yeasts used in home-brewed wine derive from the grape yeasts which occur naturally on wine grape skins and it is good practice to choose the one that most closely matches the wine you want or expect. Alternatively, you can choose yeasts which have some characteristic you need for the wine you are making. You can use a general-purpose wine yeast but it is more interesting to choose something special for each brew.

Yeasts, like most other things in home brewing, come in a bewilderingly large number of varieties: hock, burgundy, Bordeaux, Champagne, Sauternes and so on. There are also yeasts with specific properties that can, for example, produce a high-alcohol wine, or tolerate low brewing temperatures so that the subtle aromas are not evaporated away, or reduce the malic acid concentration in wines such as gooseberry or crab apple.

To achieve the correct degree of sweetness the strain of yeast you choose is important. A single must might ferment to dryness with a yeast that tolerates high concentrations of alcohol, while another, less vigorous yeast might die out, leaving the wine sweet. Information on alcohol tolerance of the various strains of yeast are readily available.

Most yeasts are bought in little sachets and most are just sprinkled on the surface of the must and stirred in after 15 minutes. However, do read what it says on the packet – you may need to prepare the yeast in a sugar solution first.

You need to prepare the must for the yeast. Since you will probably have removed any dissolved oxygen from the water by heating it you must reintroduce it just before you add the yeast. This is called aeration and permits a large colony of yeast cells to develop quickly.

It can be done by splashing the must about a bit with a spoon, or pouring the must backwards and forwards between two fermenting buckets, but I use a sterilised electric hand-held stick blender – it is quick and you get a reassuring froth on top of your must.

Once fermentation is under way and, later, the must has been transferred to your demi-john, it is essential to exclude oxygen as far as humanly possible – this encourages secondary 'anaerobic' fermentation and prevents spoilage of the wine through oxidisation.

Finings

Most wines clear eventually but it is perfectly legitimate to help them along by adding finings. This is usually done during the second racking a few days before bottling. Bentonite is a good general-purpose fining, removing the fine particles that cloud a wine by clumping them together so that they fall out of suspension. There are several others available.

In the recipes I do not mention using finings as a matter of course, but if the wine has resolutely refused to clear after 3 months in the second demi-john then that is the time to add some. Bottle a few days later.

Potassium sorbate

This is the remarkable chemical that stops yeasts breeding, thus stabilising a wine. For more details, see p.95.

Equipment

Home wine-making requires very little equipment, though this has not stopped me buying most of the contents of the home-brew store. Below is the basic shopping list. The list of 'optional' items is even longer but I will cover these extras as needed.

Weighing scales I generally use digital scales, which accurately measure anything from a few grams to several kilos.

Food-quality fermenting buckets with lids For making a typical 4.5-litre (one demi-john) batch you will need two 10-litre buckets, though they come in larger and smaller sizes if you need them. Lids can be obtained with a little grommet-filled hole in which an air lock may be inserted so that the carbon dioxide can escape without popping off the lid.

A 2-litre plastic measuring jug For pouring water over the primary ingredients.

Large saucepan For heating water.

Long-handled plastic spoon For stirring the must.

Hydrometer For measuring the specific gravity of the must.

Wine-thief A pipette for taking samples of wine or must for testing.

Trial glass A measuring cylinder in which samples can be tested with a hydrometer.

Thermometer For checking the temperature of the must.

Several demi-johns or closed fermenters These come in a standard 4.5-litre size and are usually made of glass though plastic demi-johns are also available. If you are making larger batches of wine then 25-litre plastic fermenters – 'wide-necked fermenting buckets' – are available, complete with a fitting to receive an air lock.

Several air locks and associated corks with holes An air lock is fitted to a demi-john or fermenting bucket to prevent air entering a fermentation (pictured on p.103). Water, with a few crystals of sodium metabisulphite dissolved in it, is used to form a lock, preventing air, bacteria, yeast and bugs from entering your brew and spoiling it, while allowing carbon dioxide to escape with a 'blooping' sound. This provides a clue as to how the fermentation is going; if the bubbles stop, so has fermentation.

Funnel A large plastic funnel is handy for pouring the must into a demi-john.

Nylon straining bag or muslin cloth Used to strain solid matter from the must. These are real bug traps so should always be thoroughly washed and cleaned in boiling water before and after use.

Large sieve or colander A metal or nylon sieve is used sometimes to filter out the must into a demi-john.

Siphon tube This is used to transfer must and wine from one container to another. The best siphon tubes have a rigid tube with a little cup at one end, which prevents sucking up the lees from the bottom of a fermenter or demi-john. Some have little clips for fixing the tube to a fermenting bucket or a tap at the outlet end. There are even 'self-priming' siphons which can be pumped to start the flow rather than relying on the slightly unhygienic method of sucking the wine or must with your mouth – they are cheap enough so I advise getting one of these.

An enormous number of wine bottles Any shape you like but bottles that accept corks are the best. Most wine bottles, even screw-top, will accommodate a cork. See p.105.

Corks You can buy tapered corks but I much prefer the straight ones which require the services of a corker (see p.104).

Corker For fitting corks. It is worth spending a bit of money on one of these as some cheap corkers are hard work to use.

pH meter or pH-testing strips For testing the acidity level of the wine.

Bottles and bottling

While you can buy new bottles, the home brewer has the opportunity to recycle in the most virtuous way – reusing something in its original form. I live next door to a restaurant and opposite a pub so I am blessed with a limitless supply of bottles of all shapes and sizes – my elderberry wine can live in Burgundy bottles, my parsnip in Alsatian flutes if I so wish. Sparkling wines require more serious consideration, as discussed on p.127. Reused bottles and indeed new shop-bought bottles must be scrupulously clean and sterilised. Full details of this character-building chore are given on pp.17–18. You will need to siphon your wine into the bottles.

A fitted air lock

Corking wine bottles

Corking

Screw tops have resulted in the loss of several 'vintages' and I now use only the traditional method for bottling still wines – corking. As it happens, screw-top bottles have an internal neck diameter that perfectly accepts a cork.

New corks are easy to buy and you will need a corker to insert them. This is easy and strangely satisfying, but you need to be very precise about the gap that exists between the top of the wine and the top of the bottle. Too much and the air left in the gap will damage your wine, too little and the cork will refuse to enter. The gap should be 2cm. I have devised a 'plunger' (actually a modified lipgloss container – not mine) which, when inserted into a bottle which is slightly over-filled, pushes out excess wine (stand the bottles in a tray!), leaving exactly the right gap. Corks should be new and sterilised with sodium metabisulphite – absolutely not a chlorine-based steriliser.

Things that go wrong with wine

The greatest sin for the home brewer and the commonest cause of problems is poor hygiene. It is essential to keep your brews covered and to sterilise *everything* they come into contact with. Sterilising equipment is covered in detail on pp.16–17.

The second most common cause of disaster is the wrong temperature or poor temperature control. Yeasts don't like change. If you make most home brews at a steady room temperature of around 18–20°C then things should go well. A degree or even two higher or lower and things will be fine too. Matters go awry when temperatures fluctuate too wildly. Decide on a room where the ambient temperature is a steady 18–20°C and keep your fermenting buckets and demi-johns there.

Some home brewers insist on keeping their fermenting vessels in thermostatically controlled cupboards. Less demanding of domestic real estate is a heat mat or jacket but there is no real control with these. One method, which I also use for beer, is to stand the fermenting bucket or demi-john in a larger bucket of water and submerge an aquarium heater, set to the correct temperature, in the water.

Stuck fermentations

Everything seems to be going so well – your air lock is bubbling away reassuringly and then it unexpectedly stops or slows to a crawl. Of course it may have just finished fermenting a little earlier than usual as often happens if the temperature is quite high. Test your wine to see if it is close to the final gravity you were expecting (anything from 990 for a very dry wine through to 1015 for a sweet one). Also check that the cork is snugly fitted into the neck of the bottle so that the carbon dioxide is escaping through the air lock rather than from around the cork.

Once you are assured that fermentation is indeed stuck you will need to try a succession of fixes, waiting a couple of days each time to see if it works. The first is to move the demi-john to a warmer environment, or use a heat mat or heat band. This might just give the yeast the boost it needs. The second is to give the demi-john a shake to release any live yeast from the bottom back into suspension.

Some fermentations stop because the yeast runs out of nutrients. A plain yeast nutrient is unlikely to fix things, as it does not contain the trace chemicals likely to be lacking. Use instead ½ tsp yeast energiser, such as Tronozymol.

The next fix is to rack the wine into a fermenting bucket and add a new batch of yeast. For this there are special 'restarter yeasts' which are able to cope with the shock of being dumped straight into an alcohol/sugar mix. They are normally just sprinkled over the surface, however, the best way is to mix a little warm water with 1 tsp sugar and the yeast in a jug, cover and leave until fermentation is well under way, then add 50ml of the stuck wine. Wait until this starts fermenting, then add another 100ml wine. Once this is fizzing merrily pour it back into the demi-john.

Failing these techniques I suggest reversing the polarity on the dilithium crystals and going to warp 7.5. Make it so.

Over-sweetness

Nearly all the home wines I have been offered over the years have, to my mind, been syrupy. It is all a matter of taste but if you make something for yourself and find it too sweet then too sweet it is. It may be due to a stuck fermentation, or at least a fermentation that stopped a little earlier than expected, or it may simply be down to too much sugar in the first place. If it is the latter, there is little you can do although restarting with a high-alcohol-tolerant yeast may work. Introduce it to the wine by making a small restarter batch as described above.

Blending with a dry wine is another solution. Sugar goes a long way, however, so you may need two or more bottles of dry to every bottle of sweet to form an acceptable wine. The drawback is that fermentation may very well restart (which may or may not be desirable), so return the blend to demi-johns for a few weeks before bottling.

Murky brews

With the possible exception of what is called a 'pectin haze' all wines will clear given time. 'Time' in this instance may mean a year or more. Finings are designed to remove the fine particles that cause cloudiness by making them clump together and fall to the bottom of the demi-john. If you add wine finings a week or two before bottling you should have no problems.

Some wines such as parsnip can contain a certain amount of starch. Amylase will convert starch to sugar and should be added to the must at the very beginning.

Pectin hazes are caused by pectin from many fruit and are fairly easily avoided by using pectic enzyme in the early stage, before the yeast is pitched (see p.98). After this, when alcohol is present, pectic enzyme does not work and you are stuck with a cloudy wine. In this situation (and any other!) cloudiness can be reduced by using a gravity-fed filter such as the Harris Vinbrite wine filter kit.

Ethyl acetate
This nasty affliction is easily detected by the strong smell of pear drops (or nail-polish remover) and can arise for several reasons. However, the chief culprit is the bacterium Acetobacter, which turns alcohol into acetic acid and then to ethyl acetate. It can be avoided by scrupulous hygiene and keeping your brew covered. If caught early then treat the must with a hefty dose of sulphur dioxide in the form of a crushed Campden tablet or two, followed by a 2-day rest, aeration and a restart of the fermentation. In fact, ethyl acetate is an important ester in wine, providing a fruity flavour beyond that of mere acidity. Too much, however, will take your breath away and is extremely unpleasant to drink.

Ropiness
This is an impressive fault that I have only suffered from once. The must in the fermenting bucket takes on the consistency of egg white and can pour in dollops. It is caused by Acetobacter who spend their time knitting long-chain molecules. One or two crushed Campden tablets per 4.5 litres and a good whisk will fix things – the flavour is not affected. Rest for 2 days before re-pitching the yeast.

Acetic acid
Sometimes acetic acid fails to turn into ethyl acetate and you end up with wine vinegar. If caught early enough and treated as for ethyl acetate (see above) it adds a pleasant roundness to the finished wine; if not, then it's nice on chips!

Musty flavours
Dead yeast cells fall to the bottom of the demi-john and slowly rot in a process called autolysis. This is important in achieving some subtler flavour in wines, notably Champagnes, but you can have too much of a good thing and wines must be racked into fresh demi-johns to remove them from the corpses of their creators.

Corked wines
The wet dog aroma and flavour of a corked wine is not nice. It occurs when the seal on a bottle is less than perfect, allowing oxygen into the wine. A fully inserted, sterilised cork will usually prevent problems and storing wine on its side ensures that corks do not dry out and shrink sufficiently for air to enter the bottle.

Rhubarb wine

SEASON	March–July
ORIGINAL GRAVITY	1095

I am very fond of rhubarb as it is just about the only local plant you can make fruity puddings out of early in the year. And very fruity it is too.

Early rhubarb sticks contain a lot of pectin so do be patient and give them time to grow; even with the later stems it is worth using pectic enzyme to be safe. This simple recipe produces one of the best wines I know – fruity and crisp.

Makes about six 75cl bottles

1.5kg rhubarb stalks
1.3kg granulated sugar
250ml tin white grape juice
    concentrate

1 tsp yeast nutrient
1 tsp pectic enzyme
1 Campden tablet, crushed
5g sachet Sauternes yeast

Wash the rhubarb thoroughly, then cut into 3–5mm slices (the thinner the better). A mandolin is the ideal gadget for doing this, if you are brave enough. Place in a fermenting bucket and stir in the sugar. Cover with a lid or clean tea-towel and leave for 3 days, stirring once a day.

Strain the syrup that has formed into a fresh fermenting bucket. Return the rhubarb to the original bucket, stir in 2 litres cold water and continue to stir until any remaining sugar crystals have dissolved. Leave to stand for at least an hour, then strain this into the second bucket too. Repeat with another 1.5 litres water. (Cold water is used because hot water tends to extract the pectin, making the wine cloudy.)

Add the grape juice concentrate and make it up to 5 litres with more water. Check the specific gravity and adjust if necessary. Add the yeast nutrient, pectic enzyme and crushed Campden tablet (this wine needs one). Cover and leave for 24 hours.

Aerate and pitch the yeast, then cover and leave to ferment for about 5 days, stirring every day for the first 4 days, then siphon into a demi-john and fit an air lock.

Once fermentation appears to have ceased (usually after about 1–2 months) rack off into a second demi-john.

Once the wine is clear it can be bottled if you want a fairly dry wine, or you can sweeten it as described on pp.94–5. Allow to mature for a year before drinking.

Elderberry wine

SEASON	August–September
ORIGINAL GRAVITY	1095

Many of the home wine makers I know stick to a single wine – elderberry. In a survey of home wine makers it was by far the most popular country wine and I can understand why – elderberries are the closest fruit to wine grapes in colour, juice content, tannin and acidity. The resulting wine can easily match a good grape wine.

Like wine made from grapes, elderberry wine needs to be kept for at least a year to allow the tannin to mellow before drinking. The oldest I have tried was a venerable thirty-seven years. It was light, sweet, fruity and perfect, with the tannin subdued to a mere minor note. An extra piquancy was provided by the fact that it was the last bottle of its line.

Elderberries are conspicuous inhabitants of the hedgerow, appearing from August through until late September. There is little with which they might be confused though dogwood has berries of vaguely similar appearance but in smaller bunches. A very common and embarrassing mistake is to return to pick elderberries from the same tree where you picked elderflowers in the summer. There won't be any.

Makes about six 75cl bottles

1.5kg elderberries
1.2kg sugar

1 tsp yeast nutrient
5g sachet red wine yeast

There really is nothing to this – crush the berries gently (so as not to crush the pips too much) in the bottom of a fermenting bucket with the end of a rolling pin, add the sugar then pour over 4.5 litres boiling water. The hot water will kill all the bugs so no Campden tablet is needed.

Allow to cool, check the specific gravity and adjust if necessary. Add the yeast nutrient, aerate, then pitch the yeast. Ferment for a week, stirring every day except the last, then siphon or strain into a demi-john and fit an air lock.

Rack off into a second demi-john when fermentation appears to have ceased. Bottle once the wine is clear if you want a dry wine or sterilise and sweeten as described on pp.94–5. Leave to mature for a year before drinking.

Note This is such a reliable wine to make you may wish to use the other method of obtaining a sweeter wine and use 1.4–1.5kg sugar at the beginning (see p.94).

Blackberry wine

SEASON	Late July–October
ORIGINAL GRAVITY	1095

I love elderberry wine but my favourite must be its sister, blackberry wine. It is not to everyone's taste though – some find it a little too much like blackberry cordial.

The bramble on which blackberries grow is a species-complex with over three hundred micro-species in Britain alone. This means that the blackberries they produce vary as much from plant to plant as they do from year to year. Like all foragers, I have developed a mental map telling me where the best blackberries are to be found, and also when is the best time to pick them. To be honest you do not need fat juicy blackberries to make a good wine, just those with a lot of flavour. You will certainly need to go equipped to pick them – bramble thorns are particularly vicious.

The recipe is the same as that for elderberry and there is no reason why you cannot obtain a little extra tannin by replacing one-third of your blackberries with elderberries. Blackberry and elderberry wine is a classic of the countryside. Indeed, elderberry and blackberry wines are often blended after maturity.

Makes about six 75cl bottles

1.5kg blackberries
1.2kg sugar
1 tsp pectic enzyme

1 tsp yeast nutrient
5g sachet red wine yeast

Crush the berries gently (without crushing the pips) in the bottom of a fermenting bucket with a potato masher, add the sugar then pour on 4.5 litres boiling water. The hot water will kill all the bugs so no Campden tablet is needed. Allow to cool until just warm, then add the pectic enzyme. Once cooled, check the specific gravity and adjust if necessary. Cover and leave for 12–24 hours.

Stir in the yeast nutrient, aerate, then pitch the yeast. Leave to ferment for a week, stirring every day except the last, then siphon or strain into a demi-john and fit an air lock.

Rack off into a second demi-john when fermentation appears to have ceased. Bottle once the wine is clear if you want a dry wine or sterilise and sweeten as described on pp.94–5. Allow to mature for a year before drinking.

Note For a sweeter wine you can use 1.4kg sugar at the beginning (see p.94).

Cherry plum wine

SEASON	July–August
ORIGINAL GRAVITY	1095

The cherry plum is an unregarded semi-wild fruit collected by but a few, yet a single tree will produce masses of gorgeous plums. The flavour varies considerably from tree to tree but for wine you'll need to pick the sharp-flavoured fruit, not the sweet/bland.

I have found plum wines to be a little troublesome to make. They seem to come with more than their fair share of Acetobacter. There is nothing you can do about this once it has taken serious hold and the whole lot has to go down the sink. For this reason, I recommend using two crushed Campden tablets in your fermenting must and a 48-hour wait before adding the yeast. I sometimes kill off unwanted bugs by very briefly heat-treating the must to 80°C. This should be brief as otherwise the wine tastes of cooked plums and large amounts of pectin can be released.

The wine is similar in appearance and body to a rosé but with a slight cherry flavour. This recipe will work for sharp-flavoured cultivated plums.

Makes about six 75cl bottles

2.8kg cherry plums, halved and stoned
1.3kg sugar
1 tsp pectic enzyme

2 Campden tablets, crushed
1 tsp yeast nutrient
5g sachet red wine yeast

Put the cherry plums in a fermenting bucket and mash with the end of a rolling pin. Stir in the sugar, pectic enzyme and crushed Campden tablets. Cover, then stir after 3 hours and again after 6 hours. Leave for 3 days, stirring occasionally.

Add the yeast nutrient and sufficient cold water to make up to 6 litres. Strain a little must through a muslin cloth to check the specific gravity and adjust if necessary. Pitch the yeast and ferment for a week, stirring every day except the last two.

Your must should have settled into layers: sludge at the bottom, liquid in the middle and froth/pulp on top. Place your siphon in the liquid layer and transfer this to a demi-john. If this fails, carefully strain through muslin or a nylon straining bag, stopping before the sludge. Top up any shortfall with sugar solution (1 part sugar to 3 parts water). Fit an air lock and leave until fermentation appears to have ceased.

Rack off into a second demi-john. Bottle once the wine is clear if you want a dry wine or sterilise and sweeten as described on pp.94–5. Leave to mature for a year.

Sloe wine

SEASON	September–December
ORIGINAL GRAVITY	1095

Sloes themselves are described and discussed on pp.33–4 so it is sufficient to say here that they are very easy to find provided you live in the countryside. The startling flavour of sloes comes mostly from the tannin and they contain relatively little organic acid, hence the addition of lemons to the recipe. Like the similarly tannin-rich elderberry wine, this needs a bit longer to mature than other country wines.

Makes about six 75cl bottles

1.5kg sloes
1.3kg sugar
100g raisins, chopped
Pared zest and juice of 2 lemons
½ tsp pectic enzyme
½ tsp yeast nutrient
5g sachet Bordeaux yeast

Wash the sloes, removing anything you don't like the look of, and put them into a fermenting bucket. Boil 2.5 litres water and pour it over the fruit. Once it is cool, crush the now soft sloes with clean hands.

Heat 2 litres water in a saucepan and stir in the sugar until it is dissolved, then add the raisins. Pour this into the fermenting bucket, allow to cool, then add the lemon zest and juice and the pectic enzyme. Cover and leave for 4 days.

Strain out all the solid matter and transfer the liquor to a clean fermenting bucket. Check the specific gravity and adjust if necessary.

Aerate the must, stir in the yeast nutrient, then pitch the yeast and allow to ferment for 5 days, stirring every day except the last.

Siphon into a demi-john and fit an air lock. Leave until fermentation appears to have ceased, then siphon into a second demi-john and leave until the wine has cleared completely.

Bottle if you want a dry wine or sterilise and sweeten to taste, following the instructions on pp.94–5. Give this wine at least a year, preferably longer, to mature before drinking.

Rosehip wine

SEASON	August–November
ORIGINAL GRAVITY	1095

Rosehips, like haws, are a bit of a problem for the forager – they look pretty and there are plenty of them, but what use are they? Rosehips make two appearances in the Infusion chapter (on p.43 and p.63) but, like just about everything else, they can be used to make wine. For once we do not have to worry about those troublesome seeds which sport stomach-irritating hairs – they just fall out of the wine.

While hedgerow plants like the dog rose and field rose are probably the best source for your rosehips, you can use any hip you like. If you find picking hips tiresome then choose the excellent Japanese rose, *Rosa rugosa*, as it has hips ten times bigger than the wild roses and thus is a tenth of the work to pick. Rosehips are *always* either too ripe or not ripe enough, so just pick any that are red all over and not actually rotting.

The flavour of the wine is mildly fruity with a vanilla undertone.

Makes about six 75cl bottles

1kg rosehips	Juice of 3 lemons
1 Campden tablet, crushed	½ tsp yeast nutrient
1 tsp pectic enzyme	5g sachet white wine yeast
1.3kg sugar	

Wash the hips thoroughly, removing any that are green and anything that looks nasty, then transfer to a fermenting bucket. Boil 2.5 litres water and pour over the hips. Allow to cool, then crush the hips with clean hands. Add the crushed Campden tablet and the pectic enzyme, cover and leave for 24 hours.

Heat 2 litres water in a saucepan and stir in the sugar until it is dissolved. Add this hot syrup to the fermenting bucket. When cool, add the lemon juice and yeast nutrient. Check the specific gravity and adjust if necessary.

Aerate the must and pitch the yeast. Allow to ferment for 6 days, stirring every day except the last.

Strain or siphon into a demi-john and fit an air lock. Leave until fermentation seems to have ceased. Siphon into a second demi-john and leave until the wine is clear.

Bottle if you want a dry wine or sterilise and sweeten to taste, following the instructions on pp.94–5. Allow to mature for a year before drinking.

Strawberry wine

SEASON	June–August
ORIGINAL GRAVITY	1120

Strawberry wine has a long history in Britain, the earliest recipe I have found dating back to 1745. This coincides with the introduction from France of our modern cultivated strawberry – a hybrid of two species from the Americas. I am very fond of heroic recipes so I was delighted to find one from 1832 which tells you to '*Take two hundred baskets of good ripe fruit for a barrel, and sixty-four pounds of brown sugar...*' and to add '*fourteen gallons of good white rum*'. Strawberry wine is not universally appreciated though. In 1830 the Lord Bishop of Calcutta, no less, declared:

'Hail strawberry! thou fruit divine
In any other shape than wine'

Well, I can see what he means, strawberry wine tastes so very much of strawberries. However, I heartily recommend it sweet and fortified as a dessert wine.

Strawberries lend themselves to natural fermentation and I have had considerable success letting the strawberries ferment from the native yeasts adhering to the surface. Using just wild yeasts is a high-risk strategy as you occasionally end up with the wrong yeast which may spoil the wine with off-flavours. But it is exciting to see things develop naturally and well worth trying from time to time.

This is another recipe where excess sugar is included from the start so that some is left after fermentation. If you would prefer a dry wine, or to adjust the sweetness later, then use 1.3kg sugar (see p.95). This is a fortified wine so it will be very strong. I suggest brandy as your fortifier but you could use vodka for a neutral flavour.

Makes about six 75cl bottles

2kg firm strawberries
1.5kg sugar
1 tsp pectic enzyme
½ tsp grape tannin

1 tsp acid blend or a mixture of citric,
 malic and tartaric acid
1 tsp yeast nutrient
5g sachet white wine yeast (optional)
750ml brandy

Trim the greenery from the strawberries and remove any bruised bits. If you are relying on wild yeasts do not wash them. Mash them in a fermenting bucket with a potato masher. Mix in the sugar, pectic enzyme and 1.5 litres water, cover with muslin and leave for about a week if you want the wild yeast or a single day if not.

Add another 1.5 litres water and stir thoroughly. Strain the juice through a nylon straining bag into a clean fermenting bucket, saving the pulp. Add a final 1 litre water to the pulp in the original container, stir and strain into the bucket again – remember to use scrupulously clean hands or sterilised rubber gloves.

Stir in the grape tannin, acid blend and yeast nutrient. If you are using commercial yeast pitch it now. Leave to ferment for 5 days, stirring every day except the last.

Siphon or strain into a demi-john and fit an air lock. Leave until fermentation appears to have ceased, then rack off into a second demi-john and leave until the wine is clear.

Distribute the brandy among your wine bottles and siphon in the wine from the demi-john. Leave the fortified wine to mature for at least 6 months, preferably a year, before drinking.

Crab apple wine

SEASON	September–October
ORIGINAL GRAVITY	1120

Crab apples are a bit of a trial for the forager; not because they are hard to find, but because it is not obvious what can be done with them. Crab apple jelly and…? Their problems are manifest – they are hard, have a very poor pip/skin to flesh ratio and they are very, very sharp. They do, however, make an excellent country wine.

Most of the apples thought of as crab apples are 'wildings' – offspring of discarded apple cores, and, as apples do not breed true, their characteristics are pretty random. True crab apples are always small, hard, sharp and scabby. They are a different species, though not as distinct as one would like as there has been a great deal of inter-species dalliance. For wine-making, fine considerations of parentage do not matter; any small sharp apple can be used to make crab apple wine.

A country wine is what it is – pleasant and fruity without a great deal of subtlety. I once passed a bottle round the table towards the end of a posh dinner hosted by a posh French wine company. I thought they would turn up their noses at it but they genuinely seemed to like it, commenting only that it was not particularly structured, meaning there was little complexity to the flavour – still nice though.

Makes about six 75cl bottles

2.5kg crab apples	1 Campden tablet, crushed
1.5kg sugar	1 tsp yeast nutrient
1 tsp pectic enzyme	5g sachet white wine yeast

Wash the crab apples thoroughly. Crush them in a fermenting bucket with the end of a rolling pin or however else you fancy. (Crushing apples is dealt with at length in the cider section on pp.162–4.) Stir in the sugar and leave covered for 24 hours.

Add 4 litres cold water, the pectic enzyme and crushed Campden tablet and leave for another 24 hours.

Stir in the yeast nutrient, then pitch the yeast. Leave to ferment for 6 days, stirring every day but the last. Siphon or strain into a demi-john, making up any shortfall with sugar solution (1 part sugar to 3 parts water), and fit an air lock.

Rack off into a second demi-john when fermentation appears to have ceased. Bottle once the wine is clear. Allow to mature for a year before drinking.

Mango and palm sugar wine

SEASON	All year
ORIGINAL GRAVITY	About 1100

Palm sugars from any number of palm trees have been used to make alcoholic drinks for thousands of years, even rating a mention by Pliny two millennia ago. Sago, date, coconut and, notably, sugar palm have all been employed to make a rough and ready wine, beer or spirit. The most notorious of these is arrack. As the nineteenth-century missionary Samuel Meer wrote: *'Arrack is the most injurious beverage... a single penny-worth will intoxicate a native'*. Unfortunately we cannot make arrack but if you are a native and want to find out if this is true you can buy bottles of the stuff.

Palm sugars are the dried sap of the palm, bled either from the trunk, as with birch and maple, or more usually from the unopened flower buds situated inconveniently at the top of typically very tall plants. With a massive sugar concentration of 15%, the sap was used directly to make the wine.

The jaggery goor used here is an unrefined palm sugar sold in orange/brown blocks. It has an intense taste – like molasses – with some unfamiliar flavours thrown in. The taste of the wine is as exotic as the ingredients – fruity and a little spicy. The bitterness typical of raw sugars is also present, so I suggest using white sugar for the most part to reduce bitterness from the start.

Makes about six 75cl bottles

400g jaggery goor or coconut palm sugar	2 over-ripe bananas
1kg sugar	1 tsp pectic enzyme
2 large ripe mangoes	1 Campden tablet, crushed
	5g sachet white wine yeast

Boil 4.5 litres water and dissolve the sugars to make a syrup. Peel the mangoes and slice the flesh off the stones, then crush in a fermenting bucket with the end of a rolling pin and pour on the boiling syrup. Leave to cool until just warm. Slice the bananas and add them to the fermenting bucket, then stir in the pectic enzyme and the crushed Campden tablet and leave for 24 hours.

Aerate and pitch the yeast, then leave to ferment for 6 days, stirring every day but the last. Siphon or strain into a demi-john and fit an air lock.

Rack off into a second demi-john when fermentation appears to have ceased and bottle once the wine is clear. Leave to mature for a year before drinking.

Melon fizz

SEASON	All year
ORIGINAL GRAVITY	1080

Many of us have had fun cutting the end off a marrow, mashing up the insides and putting in some brown sugar to make an alcoholic drink of doubtful worth. It is the adult equivalent of growing mustard and cress on blotting paper. Melon fizz is very similar but actually tastes nice. The fun is still there, however, as you bottle it far too soon to be safe and face the possibility of explosions.

I recently came across an unlabelled half-bottle of what turned out to be year-old melon fizz in the spare fridge I use for lager-making. I foolishly washed away the sticky stuff that had run down the side with warm water before easing off the swing-top cap. Melon fizz hit the ceiling, the window, the door, the light fitting and me. The lights fused and went out. After an hour of domestic and marital restoration I sought consolation in the small amount of melon fizz left in the bottle.

Makes about 750ml

1 ripe honeydew melon or similar
Pared zest and juice of 1 lemon

About 100g sugar
A pinch of white wine yeast

Cut the melon in half and scrape the pips, juice and fibres into a small fermenting bucket or something similar. Spoon out the flesh, mash it up and add to the bucket. Add the lemon zest and juice. Stir in some sugar until you have a specific gravity of about 1080.

Pitch the yeast, cover and leave somewhere fairly warm to ferment for a week, stirring occasionally.

Sieve and funnel into plastic fizzy drink bottles, carefully leaving the lees behind. Allow to ferment for a day somewhere warm, then keep in the fridge – but not for too long! Serve with ice.

Elderflower and gooseberry wine

SEASON	June–early July
ORIGINAL GRAVITY	1095

Every year I take to the hedgerows to gather several hundred elderflower blossoms (see p.58). Some things seem to be made for each other and elderflower and gooseberry is one such pairing. It is possible to make a straight elderflower wine but you will need to add an acidic component to provide fruitiness so it might as well be gooseberry, which is about the nearest thing we have to a grape. Fortunately their seasons more or less coincide.

Try to pick the flower heads in the morning on a sunny day, making sure that the florets are open and still yellow in the middle, and start your brew as soon as you get home so that the freshness is preserved. The florets should be stripped from the flower head with a fork, removing as many of the bitter green bits as you can.

Makes about six 75cl bottles

1kg green gooseberries, washed	1.3kg sugar
Florets from 8 elderflower sprays	1 level tsp grape tannin
1 level tsp pectic enzyme	1 tsp yeast nutrient
1 Campden tablet, crushed (optional)	5g sachet white wine yeast

Pre-freeze the gooseberries (to break down the cell walls and make the mashing process easier), then defrost and place in a ceramic mixing bowl. Crush them gently with the end of a clean rolling pin. It is important not to crush the pips too much as this will release more pectin. Once it is all nicely pulped, transfer to a fermenting bucket and pour on about 4 litres cold water. Add the elderflower florets, pectic enzyme and a crushed Campden tablet, if using, and leave for 24 hours.

Add the sugar and stir until fully dissolved. Allow the must to settle before extracting some to check the specific gravity; adjust if necessary. Add the grape tannin and yeast nutrient, then pitch the yeast. Leave to ferment for a week, stirring every day except the last. Carefully strain the must into a demi-john and fit an air lock.

Rack off into a second demi-john when fermentation appears to have ceased. Bottle once the wine is clear if you want a dry wine or sterilise and sweeten as described on pp.94–5. Allow to mature for a year before drinking.

Sparkling elderflower wine

SEASON	June–early July
ORIGINAL GRAVITY	1070–1080

This is the big one! Few self-respecting country dwellers will let the summer pass without making at least one batch of this remarkable wine. It is by far the nearest thing to Champagne you can make at home and an essential accompaniment to summer parties. There is, however, a small problem.

It is only possible to drink elderflower sparkly from a glass, not from the floor, walls and ceiling of the dining room, kitchen or garden shed. Exploding bottles are the bane of the elderflower sparkly maker and it is something that seems to happen to everyone. I read of one wine maker who kept a dozen bottles just inside the shed. Nine exploded, leaving a Hurt Locker collection of three. Since no one was prepared to approach the bottles, or indeed the end of the garden, they hit upon the rather brilliant idea of taking them out with an air rifle.

Which bottles you use has a bearing on the safety of this brew. Wine bottles will obviously have you redecorating, so something stronger is needed. You can use swing-top bottles, plastic fizzy drink bottles or Champagne-style bottles. Swing-top bottles are very good but only if you use the thick-walled variety with sturdy metal parts. Torpedo-shaped plastic lemonade bottles are just about up to it, though I was once presented with one full of elderflower fizz which had deformed into the shape of a monkey-nut and looked as though it would go bang at any moment.

Champagne bottles are designed to withstand pressure and are the most attractive solution, though it is more difficult to check how things are going and to release a little of the pressure if they are going badly. Also if they do go they produce high-velocity shrapnel, so remember to put some sandbags around your wine rack. Champagne bottles need to be corked with easy-fit plastic Champagne corks and fixed with a little cage. You can even buy shaped cups of coloured foil to make everything look the part.

There are at least three ways of making elderflower sparkly – quick and reckless, careful but not too fussy, and fussy. The second is my preferred method as it is easy as long as you keep an eye on things. The third is the 'proper' method involving a second fermentation to create the bubbles and complicated matters familiar to Champagne buffs such as remuage and disgorging (processes which enable the lees to be removed from the bottle). We are going to stick with the first two. Both are relatively low-alcohol brews and both are dry. For advice on gathering elderflowers, see p.58; for the easiest way to strip the florets from the flower heads, see p.124.

Quick and reckless recipe

This method for making sparkling elderflower is the one that can result in all that collateral damage, but it is very straightforward. I have enjoyed two-year-old elderflower sparkly made this way, so even though it is rough and ready it can keep quite well. Whenever you drink it, serve it chilled and pour carefully – there will be some sediment at the bottom of the bottle from the continued fermentation.

Makes about six 75cl bottles

800g sugar
Florets from 8 elderflower sprays
Pared zest and juice of 4 lemons

½ tsp yeast nutrient
5g sachet Champagne yeast

Dissolve the sugar in 2 litres hot water in a fermenting bucket, then top up with 3 litres cold water. Allow to cool.

Aerate and add the elderflower florets, lemon zest and juice, and the yeast nutrient. Pitch the yeast or, if you like a bit of excitement, don't. Elderflowers come ready stocked with wild yeasts and it can be interesting to see how things turn out. Leave to ferment for 6 days, stirring every day for the first 5 days.

If you did not add yeast and fermentation has not started after 3 or 4 days then it is time to give the thing a kick-start with a packet of Champagne yeast.

After 6 days of fermentation, strain the must through boiled muslin into a fresh fermenting bucket, leaving the lees behind. Cover the bucket and leave for a few hours for the dust to settle, then siphon into your bottles of choice.

Your sparkly is about ready to drink after a week, and in any case a week is a good time to check to see how things are going. You can release a little excess pressure by easing the lid off, though, as noted, this is a little tricky if you have used Champagne bottles. If you are still worried then put the lot in the fridge to slow things down a little and drink it as quickly as you can.

Tried, trusted and reasonably safe recipe

This is reliable in that it leaves a *measured* amount of sugar in the wine instead of a wildly guessed amount, ensuring that only a safe amount of carbon dioxide is produced. Still, it is worth checking to make sure things are going well. This is a bottle-conditioned wine so there will be sediment in the bottom.

Makes about six 75cl bottles

Florets from 8 elderflower sprays
Pared zest and juice of 2 lemons
900g sugar

250ml tin white grape juice
   concentrate
½ tsp yeast nutrient
5g sachet Champagne yeast

Put the elderflower florets, lemon zest and juice, sugar and grape concentrate in a sterilised bucket. Pour over 2.5 litres boiling water and stir until the sugar is dissolved. Add 2.5 litres cold water and the yeast nutrient. Leave until cool.

Aerate the must, pitch the yeast, cover and leave to ferment for 5 days, stirring every day for the first 4 days.

Strain the must into a sterilised demi-john and fit an air lock. The bubbles in the air lock should appear at about one per second. This will slow down after about a week and this is the time to test your brew with your hydrometer. Remove the air lock and carefully drop in your sterilised hydrometer. The goal is 1010. If it is not down to this level, then replace the air lock and leave your brew a bit longer. If you forget all about it and the specific gravity falls too low then add some sugar syrup.

Once the magic number has been achieved, siphon off into whichever bottles you are using. Leave for several weeks to allow the fermentation to add fizz to the wine before drinking.

A shameful cheat

Makes 1.25 litres

1 litre chilled soda water
50ml elderflower cordial

6 shots of vodka
Lemon slices

Mix, serve, don't tell anyone what you have done.

Gorse wine

SEASON	Best in April, but available most of the year
ORIGINAL GRAVITY	1095

While primrose wine and, especially, cowslip wine will have even the most rapacious of foragers worrying about conservation, the yellow of gorse fills roadside, heath and hill the country over and picking will not damage it. Gorse flowers are described on p.60. It is enough to say here that they are around for most of the year and the best time to pick is during their main flush in April while the sun is on them.

Gorse blossom makes one of the best country wines and is not to be missed. This wine does, however, need time to mature as the flavour of 'pea' (gorse is in the pea family, after all) is detectable for several months after bottling. The distinctive coconut aroma of the flowers survives the brewing and maturing processes reasonably intact and the wine as a whole is full-bodied and as rich as Xerxes.

Makes about six 75cl bottles

4.5 litres gorse flowers (½ builder's bucket, loosely packed)

1.2kg sugar (or use honey for all or part of this, using a quarter as much honey again as the sugar it replaces)

250ml tin white grape juice concentrate

Pared zest and juice of 2 lemons

½ tsp yeast nutrient

5g sachet white wine yeast

Remove any twigs and superfluous wildlife from the gorse flowers and place the blossoms in your fermenting bucket with the sugar. Pour over 2.5 litres boiling water and stir until the sugar has dissolved. When cool, add 2 litres cold water. Add the grape concentrate, lemon zest and juice and the yeast nutrient.

Check the specific gravity and adjust if necessary. Aerate, then pitch the yeast. Cover and leave for a week, stirring every day but the last.

Use a large funnel lined with a muslin cloth to strain the must into a demi-john, making sure that you leave the lees at the bottom of the fermenting bucket. Fit an air lock and leave for about 2 months.

Rack off into a second demi-john when fermentation appears to have ceased. Bottle once the wine is clear if you want a dry wine, or sterilise and sweeten as described on pp.94–5. The minimum for this wine to mature to glory seems to be 9 months.

Dandelion wine

SEASON	Late March–early May
ORIGINAL GRAVITY	1110

Dandelion wine-making is such an important part of the home brewer's calendar and so good a wine that it is one you really must try. The flower has a bitter taste but this merely imparts a pleasant astringency to the wine.

Pick the flowers in full sun, preferably in the morning (see p.65) and start your wine the moment you get home. Hold each dandelion flower by the calyx and snip off the petals with scissors into a clean fermenting bucket; if much of the green stuff ends up in your must that pleasant bitterness can become too intense but the odd few bits won't pose a problem. The recipe itself is easy, producing a rich, strong, golden wine.

As medium sweet is best for dandelion wine, I am using a little more sugar than usual, to leave some behind after the yeast has died. If you would prefer a fairly dry wine or to sweeten the wine later, then use 1.2kg sugar. See pp.94–5 for more details.

Makes about six 75cl bottles

4.5 litres dandelion petals
    (½ builder's bucket, loosely packed)
1.4kg sugar
250ml tin white grape juice concentrate

Pared zest and juice of 4 lemons
1 tsp yeast nutrient
5g sachet white wine yeast

Place the dandelion petals in your fermenting bucket and stir in the sugar. Pour 2.5 litres boiling water over the mixture, stir until the sugar has dissolved, then add 2 litres cold water. Cover and leave for a couple of days, stirring occasionally.

Strain and squeeze the floral syrup through a nylon straining bag into another fermenting bucket. Do make sure your hands are *completely* clean or use sterilised rubber gloves. Add the grape juice concentrate, lemon zest and juice and the yeast nutrient. Check the specific gravity and adjust if necessary.

Aerate, then pitch the yeast. Cover and ferment for 5 days, stirring every day except the last, then siphon into a demi-john and fit an air lock.

Rack off into a second demi-john when fermentation appears to have ceased. Bottle once the wine is clear.

Let the wine mature for a year before drinking to allow any bitterness to moderate.

Cowslip wine

SEASON	April–early May
ORIGINAL GRAVITY	1095

This recipe is included because cowslip wine is an all-time classic country wine, which, unsurprisingly, is seldom seen these days. The cowslip largely disappeared from the British countryside with the extensive ploughing of pasture and meadow after the Second World War. It has made something of a comeback as a roadside plant introduced to brighten up new bypasses and dual carriageways, but not everyone is keen on picking roadside flowers for wine, and flower-lovers may be justifiably enraged by the picking of so pretty a flower. I am fortunate in that I have my own patch, far away from any road, which no one ever sees. Still, despite the abundance of cowslips at this site, I do not like to pick more than a few blossoms and content myself with a 'pico-brew' of cowslip wine every year.

Look for cowslips in sunny locations and pick no more than half of the individual flowers that appear on each plant. Or you might prefer to replace or supplement the blossoms with those of the closely related and much more abundant primrose.

The following recipe is made in a 1-litre soft-drink container and produces barely a litre of wine. The fermenting processes in these pico-brews are very fast and complete in half the time, so I often use them when testing a new recipe.

Cowslip is indeed a lovely fragrant wine, which many have told me is the best country wine they have ever tasted… I tend to agree.

Makes about 1 litre

600ml cowslip flowers
250g sugar
Juice of 1 lemon

A pinch of yeast nutrient
1 tsp hock yeast or white wine yeast

Place the cowslip flowers, sugar and lemon juice in a sterilised container. Heat 1 litre water to 70°C, pour over the mixture and stir. When cool, aerate and add the yeast nutrient, then pitch the yeast. Cover and ferment for 3 days.

Transfer the must to a 1-litre container with a neck diameter suitable for an air-lock cork (or push a wad of cotton wool into any sized neck, making sure it does not touch the must). There is little point in racking this tiny brew – just leave it to more or less clear in the bottle then transfer it to 2 or 3 suitable-sized bottles.

Allow the wine to mature for at least 3 months before drinking.

Mead

SEASON	All year
ORIGINAL GRAVITY	Variable

The quest for alcohol has always been the quest for sugar – if you can find the latter you can make the former. Historically sugar has been difficult to obtain, certainly in pure form. Consisting of 83% sugars, honey is the nearest thing you can get to the pure stuff in nature, so it has been important in wine-making for millennia.

At heart, mead is a minimalist beverage as it contains very few ingredients: water, honey, lemons and yeast. Various flavourings are added, ginger being a favourite, but beyond a single extra ingredient the drink should really be called metheglin or any one of a score of other names, depending on the additive concerned.

Unadulterated, it is simply a wine that tastes of honey, although not as strongly as one might think. Writing in 1787, one Charlotte Mason described it as tasting like a fine, old Malaga – a dessert wine from Spain. Choosing the honey you use is a compromise between taste and cost. Some cheap honeys are perfectly pleasant, lacking only the dominant characteristics of single source (monofloral) honeys such as heather and acacia. Frankly, it is not worth splashing out on manuka honey.

Makes about six 75cl bottles

1.4, 1.7 or 2kg honey for, respectively,
    dry, medium or sweet mead
Pared zest and juice of 2 lemons
1 Campden tablet, crushed

1 level tsp Tronozymol yeast nutrient
5g sachet Lalvin D47 wine yeast
1 tsp wine finings

First stand your jars of honey in warm water to make it a little more runny or to liquefy if your honey is set. Pour 4.5 litres warm water into a sterilised container. Stir in the honey until it is completely dissolved and then add the lemon zest and juice. Add the crushed Campden tablet, stir, cover and leave for 24 hours.

Aerate, then add the yeast nutrient and pitch the yeast. Leave to ferment for 6 days, stirring every day but the last, then siphon into a demi-john and fit an air lock.

Leave until fermentation has almost ceased, then rack off into a second demi-john, adding the wine finings.

If the mead does not clear, then rack into a third demi-john. Once the wine is clear, siphon it into bottles. Allow to mature for a year before drinking.

Metheglin

SEASON	May–July
ORIGINAL GRAVITY	Variable

Metheglin (pronounced meth-*egg*-lin) is simply a flavoured mead. It predates even wine made from grapes, so it is a pity it has gone out of fashion. Traditionally it was made stronger than mead. A seventeenth-century writer says that it is '*Strong in the superlative… doth stupifie more than any other liquor, and keeps a humming in the brain*'. I can find no one who makes metheglin commercially, so if you want to hear that humming you will have to make it yourself.

The name metheglin comes from the Welsh *meddyglyn*, equivalent to *meddyg*, which means healing. There was considerable congruence between food, drink and medicine in times past and the herbal nature of many metheglins reflects this.

There are endless old recipes; the seventeenth-century *The Closet of Sir Kenelme Digby* lists several dozen with names such as 'Sir Baynham Throckmorton's Mead' and 'Mead from the Muscovian Ambassador's Steward'. An array of flavouring ingredients were used – virtually anything with a strong taste that was not poisonous (at least not *very* poisonous) and preferably good for you: watercress, fennel, ferns, liverwort, marshmallow roots, scurvy grass, cloves, borage, marjoram, flowers and so on. There is, incidentally, a third species of honey wine called 'braggot'. This is a halfway house between wine and beer as it uses hops and sometimes malt.

Broadly, metheglins fall into four categories – herby, spicy, floral and weird. You can use whatever takes your fancy – the ingredients listed below just happen to be ones I found either in my garden or foraging basket. The garden herbs and mugwort are perfectly safe but leave out the wormwood if you are of a nervous disposition.

Makes about six 75cl bottles

1.4, 1.7 or 2kg honey for dry, medium or sweet metheglin
¼ tsp grape tannin
Pared zest and juice of 2 lemons
1 Campden tablet, crushed (optional)
1 level tsp Tronozymol yeast nutrient
5g sachet Lalvin D47 wine yeast

Flavourings
About 2 tbsp chopped rosemary
2 level tsp thyme leaves
2 level tsp mugwort
½ tsp wormwood
4 bay leaves

First stand your jars of honey in warm water to make it a little more runny or to liquefy if your honey is set.

Place all the flavouring ingredients in a fermenting bucket and pour on 4.5 litres boiling water. While it is still hot, stir in the honey until dissolved. Allow to cool, then add the grape tannin, lemon zest and lemon juice. This brew should be sterile but if you want to be sure add a crushed Campden tablet. Leave for 24 hours.

Strain the liquid into a sterilised fermenting bucket. Aerate, then add the yeast nutrient and pitch the yeast. Cover and leave to ferment for 6 days, stirring every day except the last, then siphon into a demi-john and fit an air lock.

Rack off into a second demi-john when fermentation appears to have ceased and bottle once the wine is clear. Leave to mature for a year before drinking.

Variation

Spicy metheglin In place of the herbs, use 1 cinnamon stick, ½ tsp each ground ginger, mace and cloves, 1 vanilla pod and the zest and juice of 1 orange.

Birch sap wine

SEASON	March
ORIGINAL GRAVITY	1095

I must tell you straight away that there is absolutely no point in making birch sap wine. Many experienced wine makers will disagree but they are wrong. A friend of mine (clue – he wrote the introduction to this book) told me about his great success with this brew and, concerned at my unenthusiastic response, gave me a bottle to prove the point. Well, it was OK, but a little dull, as I had suspected.

With most wines the principal ingredient is there to provide the flavour or the sugar and sometimes both. Birch sap contains very little of either so it cannot do these things – it just supplies the water. To prove the point I made two small batches of wine; both were to the recipe below but one replaced the birch sap with water and a tiny extra bit of sugar to make up for the equally tiny amount in birch sap (0.7% on a good day). I gave the finished brews to some friends in a blind tasting. No one could really tell the difference and the only notable comment was that one was fuller-bodied than the other – it was the water wine. But maybe I am missing something, so here is everything you need to know about making birch sap wine.

Nothing in the forager's calendar is more seasonal than birch sap. Blackberries and wild garlic are around for months; with birch sap you have a couple of weeks, three at the most. In Dorset it is approximately the middle two weeks of March, but it can be earlier or later, depending on the weather.

I love collecting birch sap, so, apart from the odd batch of wine to remind myself how right I am, I make birch sap syrup to pour on my pancakes. I gently boil away most of the water then add sugar to make a flavoured syrup.

So how do you go about collecting this arcane ingredient? First, of course, you will need to find some mature (at least 25cm-diameter trunk) birch trees and obtain permission to drill holes in them from the owner – not always easy. And you will need more kit! A hand drill and drill bit, a bucket to collect the sap (I sometimes use a 4-litre milk container with a hole strategically cut in the side near the top), some *tapered* wooden plugs (candle waxed at the narrow end to seal them), a mallet and a large container to carry the sap home in.

You will also need some spigots or spiles. These are virtually impossible to obtain in Britain so you will have to source them online from Canada or the US where they are used for maple tapping. You *can* rig up something with tubes and pipes but I have never been able to stop it all leaking. Check, using a scrap of wood, that your plugs and spiles tightly match the drill bit you will be taking with you.

Off to the woods. Drill a slightly upward-slanting 4cm-deep hole into your chosen tree at waist height. If nothing comes out when you are halfway in, the tree is dry. Stop drilling, hammer in a plug and try another tree. After three no-shows it will be worth waiting another week. If all is well (the sap will start to trickle out as you drill), hammer in a spile, hook on your bucket through the little hole you will have made in the rim and cover it.

Come back the next day to collect your sap – if you are lucky you will get about 2–4 litres from each tree. Very carefully plug the holes – if you don't the sap will continue to flow and the poor tree may not recover from this added insult. I was having lunch in the garden of a friend of mine and admiring his rather magnificent birch tree. I mentioned birch sap wine and he told me that it was a favourite of his student days. From one tree, he told me, he extracted 15 gallons of sap in one year. It died.

Birch sap tastes *almost exactly* like water – but the freshest water you have ever tasted, with just a hint of sweetness. It does not keep very long – about 4 days in the fridge – so use it as soon as you can. Here is how you make the wine.

Makes about six 75cl bottles

4.5 litres birch sap
1.2kg white sugar
250ml tin white grape juice
    concentrate

Juice of 2 lemons
1 tsp yeast nutrient
5g sachet white wine yeast

Gently heat the birch sap in a large pan with the lid on to 75°C and turn the heat right down to keep it at that temperature for 20 minutes. Take off the heat and stir in the sugar until it is dissolved. Transfer to a fermentation bucket and allow to cool. Add the grape concentrate, lemon juice and yeast nutrient. Check the specific gravity and adjust if necessary.

Aerate, then pitch the yeast. Cover the bucket and leave to ferment for 5 days, stirring every day for the first 4 days.

Siphon into a demi-john and fit an air lock.

Rack off into a second demi-john when fermentation appears to have ceased. Bottle once the wine is clear if you want a dry wine or sterilise and sweeten as described on pp.94–5.

Leave the wine to mature for a year before drinking. The flavour? Light, fruity, with the faint piquancy of wet paper bag.

Ginger wine

SEASON	All year
ORIGINAL GRAVITY	About 1120

Ginger wine always reminds me of Christmas. My father was a sort of male matron in a psychiatric hospital. He would often be engaged in ward rounds on Boxing Day and the family would always join him. Going from nurse's station to nurse's station we would be plied with Christmas drinks. My grandmother had a famous fondness for ginger wine and was given a glass, or two, at every stop. When we were about to move on to the last ward, I noticed that she was singing quietly to herself. She stood to her full and not inconsiderable height, then, not bending a single limb, crashed to the floor like a felled Douglas fir. We carried her comatose form to the car and took her home.

It is a wine with a long history and a heyday in the Victorian period when it was consumed for 'health' reasons; well suited to a lady who was born in the 1880s.

Ginger wine hardly needs describing; it is gingery, fruity and warming down to your toes.

Makes about six 75cl bottles

40g root ginger, peeled
1.5kg sugar
100g raisins, chopped
Pared zest and juice of 2 lemons

1 tsp yeast nutrient
5g sachet white wine yeast
350ml brandy

Grate the root ginger into a saucepan, add the sugar and 4.5 litres water and boil for 30 minutes, skimming off any scum. Put the raisins into a fermenting bucket and pour over the hot liquid. Cool, then add the lemon zest and juice. Cover and leave to stand for 2 days.

Aerate, stir in the yeast nutrient, then pitch the yeast. Leave to ferment, stirring every day for 5 days.

Leave to settle for a day, then siphon or strain into a demi-john and fit an air lock.

Rack off into a second demi-john when fermentation appears to have ceased. Share the brandy out among your bottles and siphon in the wine. Allow to mature for a year before drinking.

Root vegetable wine

SEASON	All year
ORIGINAL GRAVITY	1095

It is impossible to make a palatable wine from anything in the cabbage family; you seldom hear of swede wine or turnip wine and for good reason – they taste of swede or turnip. For root vegetable wines we must turn our attention to members of the Apiaceae (carrot family) and the Chenopodiaceae (beet family), specifically carrots, parsnips and beetroot.

Carrot wine is highly thought of and parsnip wine is up there with elderberry as a bright star in the country wine firmament. The unpromisingly entitled *Cyclopaedia of Commerce, Mercantile Law, Finance, Commercial Geography and Navigation* of 1844 tells us that it *'is said to possess a finer flavour than that obtained from any other British produce'*.

Most of the early recipes are little different from the one below, though some insist on such things as 'argol of wine' and (real) isinglass – ingredients you will be hard pushed to find at your local home-brewing shop. And, of course, they invariably involve brewing industrial quantities of the stuff. One 1846 'receipt' makes it in quantities of a kilderkin (which, as Sid James would have told you, is two firkins).

Beetroot wine, on the other hand, does not seem to be much liked by anyone for the simple reason that it tastes like dirt. It does, however, have one advantage – it is extremely useful in small quantities for adding a brilliant purple to any red wine that looks a little wan.

Makes about six 75cl bottles

2kg parsnips or carrots, or (if you must) beetroot
1.2kg sugar
1 tsp pectic enzyme
½ tsp amylase
Pared zest and juice of 2 lemons

250ml tin white grape juice concentrate
½ tsp grape tannin
1 tsp yeast nutrient
1 ripe banana (for parsnip wine and optional!)
5g sachet white wine yeast

Scrub your chosen root vegetable to remove all dirt, leaving the skin on, then cut into slices about 5mm thick. Place in a large pan and add 2.5 litres water. Bring to the boil and simmer gently until soft, but absolutely not until they are falling apart (the wine will never clear if your roots are mushy).

Strain the liquid into a clean fermenting bucket. Stir in the sugar until dissolved and add 2 litres cold water. Cover and allow to cool, then add the pectic enzyme and amylase (to break down any starch) and leave for 24 hours.

Aerate the must, then stir in the lemon zest and juice, grape concentrate, grape tannin and yeast nutrient, and slice in the banana, if using. Check the specific gravity and adjust if necessary.

Aerate the must, then pitch the yeast. Cover and leave to ferment for 5 days, stirring every day except the last.

Siphon into a demi-john and fit an air lock.

Rack off into a second demi-john when fermentation appears to have ceased and leave until the wine is clear. Bottle if you want a dry wine or sterilise and sweeten to taste as described on pp.94–5. Allow to mature for a year before drinking.

Rice wine

SEASON	All year
ORIGINAL GRAVITY	1120

Rice wine is a stalwart of the home wine maker, but it is not true rice wine; that of course is sake. Rice contains little or no sugar but a great deal of starch. Starch is the basis of beer, being converted to sugars by the enzyme amylase found in malted barley. But how is the starch converted in rice? In fact it is amylase again, but rather than being produced by the rice grain it is manufactured by the fungus *Aspergillus oryzae*, known by the slightly more pronounceable name of *kome-koji*.

To make sake you prepare the rice, inoculate it with *A. oryzae*, then ferment it with yeast. To ensure authenticity it should be a special sake yeast, but it is still *Saccharomyces cerevisiae*, albeit a special strain. Both fungi are available commercially, though not particularly cheaply. Unfortunately expense would be the least of the problems for the hopeful home sake brewer. The process is slow, precise, very long and involves getting up at 3.30am to stir things. If you really want to make some I suggest taking a month off to do it.

However, I do not like to be defeated so here is a recipe which uses a few cheats (the main one in the form of amylase to convert some of the rice starch). These cheats bypass nearly all of the more complicated processes. It really, really isn't sake but a Western *homage* to this 7th Dan wine. The wine is, or should be, sweet, and sherry-like with perhaps just a hint of rice pudding, which is a good thing.

Makes about six 75cl bottles

1 tsp amylase crystals
1kg flaked rice
1 Campden tablet, crushed
500g raisins, chopped
About 600g sugar

1 level tsp Tronozymol yeast nutrient
5g sachet white wine yeast or, if you
    want to make a bit more effort,
    Wyeast Activator 4134 sake yeast

In a large container, mix 2.5 litres cold water with the amylase, then stir in the flaked rice and a crushed Campden tablet (otherwise it can start fermenting and not in a good way). Cover and leave for 5 days in a warm place, stirring occasionally. Surprisingly it does not go sticky, at least not very sticky.

At this stage check the specific gravity – it should be around 1035 (but do not worry if it is not this high, at least you tried).

Strain the liquid through a nylon straining bag or muslin into a pan, add another 2 litres water and bring to the boil.

Put the raisins and sugar into a fermenting bucket and pour on the boiling liquid, stirring until the sugar has dissolved. Allow to cool.

Add water until you have 5 litres, check the specific gravity and adjust if necessary; it should be about 1120.

Add the yeast nutrient, then pitch the yeast. Cover and keep at room temperature for 6 days, stirring every day except the last one.

Siphon or strain the liquid into a demi-john and fit an air lock.

Rack into a second demi-john when fermentation appears to have ceased and leave until the wine is clear. Bottle and leave to mature for a year before drinking.

Cider

I used to like cider a great deal until I was attacked

by five pints of scrumpy over forty years ago in the George Inn on top of Portsdown Hill near Portsmouth. The events are strangely hazy but involved a night spent in a telephone box outside the post office in Cosham. Strangely comfortable though the telephone box was, it was decades before I could go near cider again.

I have finally recovered from my experience but become rather more discerning about which ciders I will drink. Nothing too murky, too dry, too flat or too sharp and certainly nothing which delivers flavours that are unexpected.

At the risk of suffering recriminations from cider aficionados I suspect there is a certain amount of bravado in cider-making and drinking circles, which maintains that the more undrinkable a cider is, the better it is considered to be. Perhaps I am being unkind, but I am not alone in my thoughts. The great writer and gardener John Evelyn, writing in 1670, wishes to '... *prescribe a way to make a sort of cider pleasant and quick of taste, and yet wholesome to drink... For if this be Heresie, I must confess my self guilty.*'

Most people are perfectly happy with the light, often sweet, ciders that are available commercially. Around my way scrumpy is the cider of choice and if you follow the path of least resistance in making cider, scrumpy is what you will end up with.

I clearly remember the first time I attempted cider-making. Everything seemed to go well – no off-smells were produced, it did not turn to vinegar and it cleared beautifully. However, when it came to trying the stuff I thought it was pretty awful – possessing a sourness surpassed only by a bucket of under-ripe sloes and my aunt Hilda from Lowestoft. I gave some to a friend who brews a very great deal of cider and she told me that this was what cider was supposed to taste like.

If this is the sort of cider you like you are very lucky because it is easy to make. But if you prefer something which does not require so refined and experienced a palate you can make this too, with just a little more effort.

Unlike beer-making, cider-making is relatively straightforward. Indeed there is a notion that if you squeeze the juice out of some apples into a bucket and leave it covered with a tarpaulin in the shed for a few months you will get cider. While in principle this is true, the fermenting process is uncontrolled and it is impossible to make any kind of sweet or fizzy cider this way; in fact, you may well end up with cider vinegar. However, while proper cider-making requires time and care, there is nothing particularly complicated about it.

Method

Making cider is straightforward and the main stages are illustrated opposite. The apples are crushed (pic 1), then squeezed to extract the juice (pic 2). This is collected in a fermenting bucket, yeast is added and the juice is allowed to ferment (pic 3). It is then racked into a new fermenting bucket or a cask and left to mature (pic 4). If a cask is used it can simply remain there; if racked into a fermenting bucket then the cider can be bottled. Most varieties of cider follow this process, at least in part.

Types of cider

It is possible to make four main types of cider: dry and still; dry and fizzy; sweet and still; sweet and fizzy. Dry and still is by far the easiest to produce. The others require some form of intervention in the fermentation process by such methods as limiting nutrients, bottling before fermentation is complete, killing the yeast or adding sugar. Perhaps surprisingly, sweet and fizzy is the hardest.

Dry and still This is what you will end up with if you let some yeast loose on a bucket of apple juice.

Dry and fizzy There are a few ways of making this cider, all of which do the only thing necessary to make a drink fizzy – introduce carbon dioxide (see p.166).

Sweet and still No cider is completely free of sugar because some of the fruit sugars are not fermentable by yeast and remain in the cider. However, few ciders fermented out completely will be sweet enough to satisfy the modern palate, and endless methods have been devised to produce sweet cider.

Sweet and fizzy You can easily make cider sparkly and it is fairly easy to make it sweet, but it is harder to make a cider that is both at the same time. To produce the carbon dioxide for fizzy cider, you need sugar and live yeast. The problem here is that the yeast will eat all the sugar, leaving you with either a dry fizzy cider or a flat, stronger cider. There is no easy answer to this. Most of the sweet fizzy stuff in supermarkets is passed through industrial-grade filters to remove all the yeast so that fermentation does not restart, and sugar is added. Carbon dioxide is then injected into the cider under high pressure. Since no one will have all the necessary equipment hanging around in their kitchen, a compromise must be reached.

There are several ways of making cider sweet and fizzy at home and, while none of them are perfect, an acceptable sweet fizzy cider is obtainable.

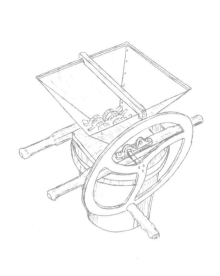

Crushing the apples in a scratter

Fermenting the apple juice in a fermentation bucket

Pressing the apples to extract the juice

Siphoning or racking the cider into a cask

Ingredients

By a very long way the principal ingredient is apple and many craft cider makers resolutely refuse to add anything else, viewing any such practices as crimes against nature. However, for those of us who have not reached this level of purity there are a number of ingredients that can be usefully added without too serious a damage to our karma.

Apples

Making cider is rather like making grape wine – ideally you only need one ingredient. With cider it is, quite obviously, apples. The question is which sort? In truth it should be one or more of the many varieties of specially developed cider apples and most of the cider makers I have spoken to view the use of any other variety with an incredulous shake of the head. While cider apples are easy to come by in West Dorset they can be a little scarce elsewhere, but it is perfectly possible to make a very acceptable cider with dessert apples provided that they are accompanied by cooking apples or, best of all, crab apples. Of course, if you are really keen and have the space in your garden it is possible to plant your own cider apple trees, although ideally they should be of more than one variety.

Crab apples

Clearly people did not go to the enormous and time-devouring trouble of developing special breeds of apple for nothing, so what do cider apples have that your average French Golden Delicious lacks? The really big difference is that cider apples are more fibrous and thus easier to press – they do not just squidge out of the press as apple purée. There is a little more to it, of course – cider apples contain a good balance of high sugar, high tannin and low acidity.

There are many, many varieties of cider apples and they are divided into four different types, depending on their balance of sugar, tannin and acid. These types are 'sweet', 'bittersweet', 'sharp' and 'bittersharp', each used and usually blended to provide a variety of ciders. The waters are muddied slightly by there being such fine distinctions as 'mild bittersweet', 'medium bittersharp' and so on. 'Bittersweet' is the most important of the cider apple types, having high sugar, high tannin and low acid levels.

The names of cider apples are charming: 'Broxwood Foxwhelp', 'Captain Broad', 'Collogett Pippin' and 'Hangdown' among them. I inherited what my neighbour told me was a Tom Putt when I moved into my house. Unfortunately it succumbed to my gardening expertise and is no more.

As I have indicated, you do not need to use cider apples to make cider – any apple will do the trick – but it is as well to use a blend of different varieties to balance out those three important components – sugar, tannin and acid. Any sweet dessert apple, such as Cox's or Russet, will make a good cider but is best if balanced with 30% crab apples, which will provide the tannin and some of the acidity the dessert apples lack. Crab apples are also very fibrous, a characteristic which will help if you are using a press. Failing crab apples, then use 40% cooking apples, such as Bramley.

It is essential to do a 'test juice' using the apple or apples you have chosen in the proportions you intend to use them. This will give you an indication of the levels of sugar, tannin and acid you will achieve. A hydrometer will be needed to check the sugar level and a pH meter or testing strips for the acid. With tannin you will just have to taste it, see p.157.

Sugar

Generally speaking, sugar is not added to 'proper' cider even though there is a great deal of evidence that it was common practice among many cider makers in the past. According to William Ellis (*The Complete Cyderman*, 1754), it made '*the best of cyder*'. Many modern, commercially produced ciders are little more than fermented sugar syrups; cider can be sold as cider with as low as 35% apple content. The reason that proper craft ciders have no sugar added is that there is enough sugar in the juice to give them an absolute volume of alcohol of 8.5% (maximum). Any higher than this and the cider is classed as a wine with a much higher UK duty.

Sugar is frequently added to increase sweetness at the end of the fermenting process. Cider left in peace will normally lose all trace of sweetness over time, either in the fermenting vessel or, more dangerously, in the bottle (you get carbon dioxide as well from continued fermentation). If you add sugar to fermented cider it will just carry on fermenting and the desired sweetness will not be attained. For this reason, the sugar is usually added just before the cider is consumed.

Yeast

Many cider makers do not use a proprietary yeast – it is something that is freely available in the air, sometimes on the surface of the apples and often just everywhere inside the building in which cider is habitually made. However, I recommend pitching yeast into your apple juice to get fermentation off to a flying start. Cider yeasts, some of them rather expensive, are available but there is no reason why a white wine or Champagne yeast could not be used. For more information on yeast and fermentation, see p.13.

Yeast nutrient

Some cider makers add yeast nutrients to ensure that fermentation is vigorous and continues until all the sugars are gone. However, they are not really necessary and other producers often go to considerable lengths to remove nutrients to stop fermentation early.

Pectic enzyme

Apples contain a hefty 1–1.5% pectin so it is little surprise that cider often fails to clear. Pectic enzyme added before fermentation will prevent the 'pectin haze', though to be honest not many people bother with it as most ciders clear with time. However, it is well worth using if you are making perry, which is notoriously difficult to clear.

Malic acid

If you have your blend of apples slightly wrong then you may find that the juice is not acidic enough. This will produce a cider that may be rather bland but, worse still, prone to infection. I strongly recommend rectifying this by adding some juice from very acidic apples. Adding the natural acid of apples, malic acid, will also work; it is just not something that craft cider makers do very often. Deciding on the level of acidity is something that can be done by taste with a little experience, but an accurate pH meter is a great deal of help here. Being terribly keen on filling the house with kit, I bought one and have not regretted the outlay – it is very useful in wine- and beer-making too. See Campden tablets (opposite), which covers this matter in more depth.

Tannin

Tannin provides bitterness to cider but also gives 'bite' or 'mouth-feel'. The latter comes from its astringency. Tannin binds components of your saliva to increase the friction within your mouth – really. If you have chosen your apple varieties with care you should have plenty of tannin in your juice, but a juice made entirely from dessert apples is likely to be low in tannin and you will need to add some in powder form – 1 tsp tannin to every 4.5 litres juice is usually enough.

Campden tablets

Campden tablets (or more precisely the sodium metabisulphite from which they are made) release measured amounts of sulphur dioxide into wines and ciders and are more important in cider-making than in any other aspect of home brewing. Their primary purpose is to kill off unwanted yeasts and bacteria before fermentation with the desired yeast is started.

Unfortunately there is no simple way of knowing how many Campden tablets to use. Every 5 litres of juice will require from three tablets down to none at all. This depends on the acidity of the juice, as high acidity suppresses bacterial action on its own. If you have a pH meter it is easy:

pH OF THE APPLE JUICE	NUMBER OF CAMPDEN TABLETS NEEDED
Below 3.0	None (but your cider will be very acidic)
3.0–3.3	1
3.3–3.5	2
3.5–3.8	3

This assessment relies on a good pH meter or narrow-range (2.8–4.4) pH-testing papers, which are much cheaper. For a pH above 3.8 you really need to increase the acidity with an acidic apple juice or some malic acid.

If you are worried about using sulphur dioxide in something you are going to drink then I must reassure you that very little will be left by the time the cider is consumed and the majority will have dissipated within 24 hours. It is also highly traditional – in the past cider barrels were invariably sterilised by placing sulphur candles in them before filling with the soon-to-be-fermented juice. Of course there are always other views and some cider makers I know refuse to use it at all, relying on the acidity alone. They seem to get by without it provided the pH is 3.8 or lower, so perhaps the home cider maker can too. However, the inadvertent manufacture of cider vinegar is a fate much suffered by home cider makers and I recommend the use of Campden tablets unless you have religious objections.

Equipment

If you take to cider-making you will probably want to buy all the kit – including an apple crusher or 'scratter' and an apple press (pictured on p.161), but for those starting out it is possible to make a gallon or two of cider using standard home wine-making equipment and a kitchen gadget or two.

For small cider batches

For basic, small-volume cider-making of a gallon or two (4.5–9 litres) you will need:

Electric juicer This can produce a stream of juice quite quickly. The really cheap models are not quite man enough but you will not need catering quality.

Two 10- or 15-litre fermenting buckets These come complete with lids, one of which should have a hole and grommet to accommodate an air lock.

Nylon straining bag This will enable you to squeeze the last drop of juice from the pulp left over from the juicer.

Hydrometer This is used for measuring specific gravity (see p.15).

pH meter or narrow-range pH-testing strips Essential for checking the acidity level of the juice.

Siphon Used for transferring the juice or cider from one container to another.

Demi-john You will need a standard 4.5-litre demi-john. Most are glass, though plastic ones can also be found.

Air lock and cork This is standard wine-making equipment. The air lock fits securely into a hole in the cork. Air locks are available in a number of designs. Fortunately they are now made of plastic, not glass, the latter having resulted in many a trip to A&E.

Bottles or a cask These are needed to store the end product. Strong swing-top bottles are the easiest to use if you want to bottle your cider. Although small and rather romantic wooden casks are available I suggest using the boring plastic variety despite their evident lack of authenticity. It is difficult to sterilise wooden casks and they sometimes allow air into the cider which can quickly spoil it. It is also possible to rack and leave your cider in a corked demi-john.

Apple crusher or scratter

For large cider batches

If everything has gone well with your attempts at making small batches of cider, or if you want to plunge straight in and start making oceans of the stuff, you will need some decidedly industrial equipment in addition to a few of the items listed above. The latter are repeated here.

Fruit masher Also known as an apple mill and, charmingly, as a scratter (pictured on p.159).

25-litre (or larger!) fermenting bucket This must be complete with lid.

25-litre wide-neck fermenting vessel This comes with a hole in the top to accommodate an air lock. The screw-on lid helps to protect your cider better than a standard fermenting vessel.

Apple press These range from small aluminium and steel presses, through cast iron and wood to agricultural constructions, which need their own shed. My friend Ross owns the largest 'domestic' press I know of. It is an ancient Somerset 'mobile' press made of oak and iron and is about the size and weight of a Ford Transit van loaded with used car batteries. He is very proud of it.

Siphon Used for transferring the juice or cider from one container to another.

Nylon straining bag This will enable you to squeeze the last drop of juice from the pulp, though one is generally not needed.

Hydrometer Required for measuring the specific gravity (see p.15).

pH meter or narrow-range testing strips To check the acidity level of the juice.

Air lock You will need one that fits securely in the top of your fermenting vessel.

Barrel While wooden ones are available it is easier to use the plastic variety. These come most often in 10- and 25-litre sizes, ready fitted with a tap and a screw cap in which there is a very simple carbon dioxide escape valve. A wide-neck wine fermenter into which an air lock can be fitted may be used instead provided you only want a fairly still cider. You can also buy a 'plastic bag in a box' to keep still cider in. These desperately unromantic containers prevent air coming into contact with your cider and spoiling it. I have also seen a 'plastic bag in a barrel', which just about tackles the unromantic bit.

Apple press

Juicing apples for cider

You will need about 10 kilos of apples for every 7 litres of juice. The volume of cider produced will be a little less than the amount of juice. All the varieties of cider – dry, sweet, still, fizzy – start with the same juice.

Preparing the apples

Using clean apples is essential in making cider. First pick over the apples, removing bad bits (the odd, clean bruise is OK) and anything that you do not like the look of. Wash them thoroughly in cold water, then wash them again, this time with a crushed Campden tablet added for every 5 litres water. Drain the apples and rinse.

Juicing small batches

If you are making a small batch of a gallon or two, the simplest way to juice the apples is to use a domestic fruit juicer. These fiendish devices mash the apples and extract the juice in one noisy operation. They partially purée the fruit, throw the juice centrifugally through a sieve into one container while the (fairly) dry pulp is flung into another. The ordinary domestic ones are just about powerful enough to do this. Mine will produce juice for a gallon of cider (4.5 litres) in about 15 minutes, though it does start to complain a bit towards the end. The 'waste' pulp still contains some juice and I squeeze it through a nylon bag to extract as much as I can.

The juice should be collected in a fermenting bucket and kept covered.

Juicing large batches

To make much more than a gallon, you will need to crush and press the apples separately. Before you start, extract the juice from a few apples (a blender and nylon bag will do the trick) to test for specific gravity and acidity. The SG should be around 1050–1055; much lower and the resulting alcohol content will be too low for the cider to keep. If the SG is not high enough you must reassess the apples you are using and introduce a sweeter variety. Similarly test the acidity with your pH meter or testing strips and adjust as suggested on p.156.

Milling, crushing or scratting apples has occupied many inventive minds over the years. Whatever you use, you should end up with a coarse pulp and not a purée, which would be impossible to press. The most primitive method is to pound the apples in a fermenting bucket with a substantial piece of wood until you get a coarse pulp. It is very, very hard work.

The method favoured by men with sheds is to put the apples into a fermenting bucket and use a homemade or proprietary (but always deadly) rotating blade attached to an electric drill by a shaft. You can even buy special lids with a bushed hole in the top for just this purpose. The trick is to ease the blade down, not plunge!

Apple juice running from the press

Garden shredders are occasionally pressed into service with varying degrees of success. But for pressing juice in large quantities you really need to move away from Heath Robinson devices and buy a proper apple mill. Mine is my pride and joy and it sits on top of my press so that the pulp goes straight in. Depending on your mill it can be worth passing the pomace (apple pulp) through the apple mill a second or even third time.

With several gallons of pomace at your disposal you now need something to squeeze the juice out. If you just squeeze pomace all you will get is pomace, so some way must be found to leave dry pulp behind while allowing the juice to flow free.

Traditionally this was, and still is in my part of the world, done by making a 'cheese'. The pomace is spread on the bed of the press and a layer of straw placed on top. Another layer of pomace is added then more straw, the straw layers being neatly tucked in each time. If you put an industrial hydraulic press on a cider cheese it would just burst, so the whole pressing process is done slowly over several hours, a turn of the screw being made at well-spaced intervals.

You might be pleased to know that you do not need to make a cheese, you just put your pomace into a press with slatted or perforated sides and turn the screw. You will still need to take your time as the juice can only be extracted slowly. A 5-minute rest between turns of the screw is about right.

As the pressed 'cake' will still contain sugar no matter how hard you squeeze, it is worth breaking it up and adding 1 or 2 litres of water to every 5 kilos of cake, then re-pressing and adding to the rest of the juice. Second-press juice will be a fairly thin liquor but, provided your apples are sugar-rich, worth the (considerable) effort. All the juice should be collected in a suitably sized fermenting bucket and kept covered. If your juice contains very much solid material then arrange a large nylon straining bag in the fermenting bucket to catch it. Keep the juice covered as much as possible. Always allow plenty of room – about 10cm – above the surface of the juice to provide space for the froth which comes with fermentation.

My most serious problem at this point is not drinking the juice. The stuff you get straight out of the press before it has oxidised has to be tried to be believed – it is wonderful. It is also surprisingly sweet; even crab apples produce a perfectly acceptable apple juice and with apples such as Russets it is almost syrupy.

Testing sugar level and acidity

Test the specific gravity using your hydrometer (see p.15) and make a note of it in your logbook. It should be at least 1050. If you have done a test batch you should not have any unpleasant surprises, but if you do there will be nothing for it but to find some sweet apples and add the juice from them.

Test the acidity of the juice using a pH meter or narrow-range pH-testing strips. Again make a note in your logbook.

Dry still cider

Whichever and however much cider you wish to make, you will need to follow the instructions for making a dry still cider up to at least partway through the fermentation. The exception to this is one of the processes used for making sweet cider – keeving – described on p.169.

Ingredients
- **Apple juice**
- **Campden tablets**
- **Pectic enzyme**
- **Yeast**

Add crushed Campden tablets to the apple juice in the fermenting bucket (see pp.162–4) according to the table on p.157, to kill off any unwanted yeasts and reduce the chance of bacteria infecting your cider. Now add ½ tsp pectic enzyme for every 5 litres of juice. Cover and leave for at least 24 hours.

Aerate the juice to the point of frothiness, cover, allow to settle for an hour or so, then pitch the yeast. Leave to ferment for 5 days.

By now the fermentation will be mostly complete and the specific gravity down to about 1005. For a small quantity, siphon into a demi-john and fit an air lock. For a large quantity, siphon the cider into a wide-necked fermenting vessel and fit an air lock if bottling, or siphon into a cask if not.

Cider is, unsurprisingly, usually made in the autumn and it is at temperatures typical of the season that it is fermented. A steady 15°C will do the trick, though it is a fairly forgiving process.

Some lees will continue to form but this can be a good thing as it will help to reduce acidity to palatable levels. A quite different type of fermentation may take place at some point over the next few months. It is called malo-lactic fermentation and is caused by a bacterium called Lactobacillus. It converts some of the malic acid into the considerably less potent lactic acid, making the cider much more palatable. It is an unreliable fermentation – sometimes it happens and sometimes not. The lees at the bottom can help because as the dead yeast cells break down (autolyse), nutrients are released to encourage malo-lactic fermentation.

There is very little unfermentable sugar in cider and the specific gravity will eventually go down to below 1000.

Your cider will be ready to serve from the cask or to siphon into bottles in about 4 months, though longer is better. If you are bottling, keep the air space at the top of the bottle to a minimum. Cider turns to vinegar for a pastime if it is exposed to air so casks too should be well sealed. Cider keeps pretty indefinitely but is generally consumed within a year.

Dry sparkling cider

I can't think of a reason why anyone would make a dry sparkling cider; it is acidic enough already without adding the extra tang that carbonic acid provides. However, if sparkling dry cider is what you want, the usual method is the one also used in beer- and wine-making – bottle or cask conditioning. This is the process of adding more sugar and allowing the yeast to start fermenting again and produce carbon dioxide. If this fermentation takes place in a cask or bottle the carbon dioxide will be retained in solution and the cider will become fizzy.

Add sugar to the cider after a month in the fermenter or cask (see p.165), stirring it in with a long-handled spoon. You will need 7g to every 1 litre and I suggest caster sugar, which dissolves more easily.

If the cider is to be left in the cask there is nothing more to do, but if it is to be bottled leave it for 24 hours to settle, then siphon into Champagne bottles. There will be a small layer of dead yeast at the bottom of every bottle, so chill upright before serving and pour carefully.

Adding carbon dioxide

Artificially adding carbon dioxide is a second possibility if you wish to make a dry sparkling cider. Fitting a carbon dioxide cylinder to the top of a barrel of dry cider will fizz it up to some extent, with the added benefits of making it easier (or at least quicker!) to draw and filling the headspace with carbon dioxide rather than air which can spoil cider.

Sweet still cider

The time-honoured and simplest way to make sweet still cider is to add sugar or sweet apple juice to a dry still cider before serving. If you add sugar in any form to cider that is much less than a year old you risk setting off the yeast in it again. This will not only reduce the amount of sugar in the cider, which is what you are trying to increase, but will also produce carbon dioxide which could easily reach explosive levels in a bottle. This is why extra sugar should be added to cider at most a day or two before serving and the cider then preferably kept in the fridge.

Sweetening with sugar

Decant your dry cider (made to the method given on p.165) into a jug and stir in some caster sugar until it achieves the level of sweetness you want. The effect this simple addition has on dry homemade cider is quite astonishing. Long before you taste any sweetness, you will notice a drop in acidity as the full, wonderful flavour of the cider emerges.

Sweetening with apple juice

Whenever I make cider I keep some fresh apple juice back to drink or to use for sweetening cider. In my opinion it is the very best way to sweeten cider. Apple juice does not keep very long in the fridge (2 weeks maximum) so it needs to be either frozen in plastic tubs or bottled. If you bottle apple juice then you will need to pasteurise it too, to prevent it fermenting – and turning into cider.

Pasteurising apple juice Fill some swing-top bottles with apple juice, leaving a 2cm gap at the top, and close the lids loosely. If you wish to be doubly sure, add about a quarter of a crushed Campden tablet for every litre of juice.

Stand the bottles upright on a tea-towel you are not fond of in a very large saucepan. If you are a beer maker you will have an industrial-sized stockpot, which is just the thing. Fill three-quarters of the way to the top of the bottles or the saucepan, whichever is the shorter, with cold water. If the pan lid does not fit on top, drape some more tea-towels over it and the bottles to keep the heat in. Put the pan on the hob and turn on the heat, making sure you don't set fire to the tea-towels. Once it reaches a temperature of 70°C, lower the heat and maintain the temperature as best you can for 20 minutes. Turn off the heat, clip the lids shut, replace the lid or tea-towels and allow to cool.

Sweetening with non-fermentable sugars

Of course, fermentable sugars such as sucrose, fructose and glucose are not the only sugars; there are others that yeast cannot consume because they lack suitable enzymes. Chief among these is lactose, the sugar found in milk. If you add lactose to cider it will taste sweet, but it will not start fermenting again. Lactose is not quite as sweet as sucrose (the sugar you buy in packets) so you will need to use a little more than you might expect.

How sweet you want your cider to be is a matter of taste so you need to make a test sample. Weigh out 200g lactose. Take 500ml of your dry finished cider (see p.165) and stir in small quantities of lactose until you are happy with the level of sweetness. See how much lactose you have left. Do the maths for the quantity of cider you wish to sweeten and stir in the calculated amount to your cask or fermenter with a long-handled plastic spoon.

Unfortunately yeast is not alone in being unable to digest lactose: the majority of adults in the world are unable to do so either, having lost the enzyme (lactase) needed at weaning, though most northern Europeans do retain it. This issue may limit your use of lactose in cider; certainly, if you are lactose intolerant you can forget it, and if you are not then do warn people before passing round the bottle.

Fortunately, there are other sweetening agents such as sorbitol that can be used and these are available from home-brew suppliers.

Keeving

The most sophisticated way of obtaining a sweet cider is to employ the ancient technique of keeving. This limits the activity of yeast by simply starving it to death – not by allowing it to run out of sugar, but by reducing the amount of other nutrients instead.

Wild yeasts from the apples, air or, more commonly, the equipment begin to ferment the juice very slowly, forming a brown cap on the top of the juice which takes some nutrients with it. At the same time the pectin binds on to more nutrients and they sink together to the bottom. Because this method is popular in France, all these effects and processes have French names; the last one, unfortunately, is called *défécation*.

The following information comes courtesy of my friend Nigel from Bridge Farm Cider in Somerset (where else?), who tells me there is nothing to it. See what you think.

For keeving it is best to use bittersweet varieties of cider apple, preferably taken from mature orchards which produce fruit that is low in nutrients and high in tannin. If you are using dessert apples, they will need to be blended with around 30% crab apples though this is a difficult enough process already and using dessert apples at all is not going to help.

The process should begin on a cold day (when the temperature is about 5°C), and when it looks as though it will be succeeded by another 6 such days (or you clear out the fridge and use that).

Prepare the pomace as for dry still cider (see pp.162–4) but instead of pressing it immediately, store it in a fermenting bucket for 24 hours. This enables the pectin to seep out of the apple cells and into the juice.

Press the pomace and run the juice into a fermenting bucket as usual. Add half the number of crushed Campden tablets that you would have used for a dry still cider (see p.165).

Cover the fermenting bucket for a week while the magic happens. You should see a brown cap forming on top of the juice within a day or so. If the fermentation becomes vigorous and the brown cap disappears to form a frothy white cap then all is not well and you will have to continue with this batch as a normal dry cider.

All being well after the week's fermentation, you will be left with a nutrient-poor but sugar-rich juice. The juice is siphoned, carefully avoiding both sediment and froth, into a second fermenting bucket and allowed to ferment normally (see p.165), though fermentation will be slow because of the lack of nutrients. Fermentation will stop before all of the sugar has been metabolised due to lack of nutrients. The cider should be racked again to remove it from the sediment at about 2 months. The final gravity should be about 1015. Bottle or leave in cask. Over to you.

Sweet fizzy cider

The easiest and most reliable method for making sweet fizzy cider is to sweeten a dry fizzy cider, using sweet apple juice or sugar syrup (100g sugar dissolved in every 150ml water and brought to the boil). It is best to make the sugar syrup as adding sugar crystals would result in a rush of carbon dioxide from the cider. Adding sugar will normally have to be done immediately before serving by decanting the cider into a jug first.

Adding carbon dioxide to sweet still cider

You could do things the other way round and add carbon dioxide to cider sweetened by keeving or the addition of unfermentable sugar.

For a small quantity this will have to involve a domestic soda-maker, but it is possible to fit a carbon dioxide cylinder to a cask, which will fizz up the cider quite well (see p.166).

A more serious approach is to restart the fermentation of a cider that has been sweetened with non-fermenting sugar (see p.168) by adding sugar that *will* ferment. Stir 7g ordinary white sugar or glucose (fermentable sugar) for every 1 litre of cider into your cask or fermenting vessel of cider using a long-handled plastic spoon. With the cask there is nothing more to do, save keeping an eye on things. With a fermenting vessel, wait for a day or so to see if fermentation has restarted and then bottle immediately in Champagne bottles. There will be a small layer of dead yeast at the bottom of every bottle so chill upright before serving and pour carefully.

Things that go wrong with cider

If your sugar level (specific gravity) and acidity level are correct and you are careful about cleanliness, your cider will turn out healthy. Keeping it healthy is another matter. Exposure to air is the commonest cause of problems, cider vinegar being the end result. If you are siphoning into bottles, then do so carefully, not splashing the cider around and introducing air. If you are not bottling then the bag-in-a-box is ideal for allowing you to draw off cider without introducing air. A cask – where you need to let in air to draw out cider – is fine if you are going to drink the lot quite quickly, but if you want to keep it for several weeks I suggest fitting a carbon dioxide cylinder, which will fill the headspace with carbon dioxide, not air. It will make the cider a little fizzy, but that is not necessarily a bad thing.

I've never known a stuck fermentation in cider – apple juice seems to *want* to be fermented – but if you ever get one you will have a naturally sweet cider. Provided the specific gravity is not above 1015, it should contain enough alcohol to keep.

Perry

Even experienced cider makers find perry difficult to produce. Pears do not press well, clarity is very difficult to achieve and the pear juice can quickly become infected with Acetobacter, which produces acetic acid, in turn producing ethyl acetate. This is nail-varnish remover and the smell is overpowering. Unless the smell of ethyl acetate is only mild (ethyl acetate is the smell of pear drops so a little can only be a good thing), there is nothing to be done other than throw the whole batch away.

True perry, like true cider, is made from fruit bred for the purpose. As with cider apples these pears have interesting names, with 'Late Treacle' and 'Dumbleton Huffcap' leading a strong field in the silliness stakes. Unfortunately they are not so easily replaced with dessert varieties as cider apples are, because dessert pears lack sufficient acid and tannins to make a good perry. And, of course, they are pretty hard to come by in most parts of the country.

If you are using dessert pears you will need to use those that are fairly firm so that the juice may be extracted. It will also be necessary to add in the missing acids and tannin.

Although acidity can be increased by using malic acid, a more natural way is to use a proportion of crab apples in your perry. When using dessert pears to make perry, one-third of the pomace should consist of crab apple. However, you will need to experiment with the pears and crab apples you have to hand to achieve the correct level. Test for acidity using a pH meter or narrow-range pH-testing papers as for cider (see p.155). The bonus with crab apples is that they contain considerable amounts of tannin.

As anyone who eats pears will know, their sugar level is all over the place, from almost none at all to sickly sweet, so choosing your dessert pears and their degree of ripeness is important and more attention than usual is needed when testing the juice with a hydrometer.

The process for making a dry still perry is pretty much the same as for making a dry still cider and it can be sweetened and carbonated in the same way (see pp.165–170). However, there are a few differences.

Whether using dessert or perry pears, it is important to double the number of Campden tablets you would normally use when sterilising a pomace for cider. This is because fairly high levels of acetaldehyde in pears inhibit the effect of sulphur dioxide, allowing Acetobacter to grow. Leave the pomace for 2 days instead of the usual 24 hours after the addition of the Campden tablets to give the sulphur dioxide time to dissipate.

Since the clouding effect of pectin is more of a problem with pears than with apples, make sure you do not forget to add pectic enzyme.

Adding other fruit or flowers to cider

If you like the flavour of certain fruits or the perfume of certain flowers there is no reason not to add them to your cider. Fruit-flavoured ciders have become quite popular, with several on sale in shops. Many fruits have been tried, from strawberry to pomegranate, raspberry to elderberry. The favourite, and the one I can heartily recommend, is blackberry cider. If you can make a sweet version, it is like blackberry and apple crumble in a glass. The only other one I have attempted is elderflower and I liked that too. For anyone who likes elderflower wine *and* cider, it is a delight.

Ending up with 25 litres of flavoured cider you do not like would be a minor tragedy, so start by making a small batch; just a demi-john will do. Even more cautiously you could add a little of the fruit juice or an infusion of flowers to a finished cider to see if it is likely to be worth making.

Blackberry cider Follow the recipe for cider on p.165. Stir in 100ml blackberry juice for every 5 litres of the freshly made apple juice.

Elderflower cider Follow the recipe for cider on p.165. Stir in the florets from 8 elderflower heads for every 5 litres of the freshly made apple juice.

Mulled cider

We cannot leave cider without mentioning this mainstay of Christmas, or more properly of Twelfth Night. Wassailing is still alive in my part of the world and you have not lived until you have stood in a circle round an apple tree singing…

> *Stand fast root, bear well top,*
> *Pray God send a good howling sop:*
> *On every bough, twigs enow,*
> *On every twig, apple big.*

Our ancestors employed any method that might encourage their apple trees to be fruitful – singing and banging drums is as good an idea as any. It would seem rude to have such a party without some of the fruits of the tree and, since Twelfth Night is in January, a warm drink is bound to be better than a cold one.

To make enough to serve 4, pour 1 litre still cider into a saucepan and add a glass of good apple juice if you like. Add 6 cloves and 4 cinnamon sticks, cover and bring slowly to the boil. As soon as it starts to simmer turn off the heat and add 200ml sloe gin (optional, but highly recommended) and 1 or 2 sliced oranges. Taste, and add a little honey or sugar if you want. Serve straight away… by a log fire.

Beer

Having been brought up on a bedtime egg-cupful of Little Bricky throughout my formative years it took me a long time to actually learn to like beer. Little Bricky was a barley wine from our local brewery, Brickwoods in Portsmouth, and nasty enough to put most people off beer for life. For many years I was a dedicated lager drinker, eschewing the heavier flavours of beer. But at the behest of incredulous friends I made valiant and ultimately successful attempts to appreciate the finer points of beer. Now I can hold my own at CAMRA meetings, talking knowledgeably about Munich malt, lauter tuns and diastatic power, and sincerely I think I have finally recovered from all those Little Brickies.

The great thing about making your own beers is that you can make them to your own taste. I regularly make my four favourites and start to get nervous if stocks run low. Even though I am content with these, I still experiment when a friend suggests a recipe or I have a bright idea. I suggest that you try a few of the recipes in this chapter, then stick to the ones you like. I give the basic theory and techniques of beer-making and recipes for a wide range of types – from beer you can give to toddlers, to stuff you can use to fix the shed roof.

The word 'beer' is a slippery creature whose meaning changes from person to person and from age to age. Historically it has been used for any undistilled brew which does not involve grapes. If it had grapes in it then it was wine, if it did not then it was called beer or wine fairly interchangeably (the strong beer called barley wine being a small memorial to the old usage). The difference between beer and ale is similarly movable. Although both are made from malted barley or other cereal, beer (in the sense of something made from cereals) was an ale which used hops instead of, or in addition to, the various traditional herbs which had been employed previously. Now ale seems to have taken on the meaning of 'a good beer', presumably in contrast to boring, ordinary beer.

The main topic here is beer in the sense of an ale with hops but I will also touch on ale in the older sense of a grain-based fermentation flavoured with herbs. In addition I have some beers in the *ancient* sense that could arguably be called wine but are still commonly referred to as beer, nettle beer being an example. Things could not be more clear.

A glance at any book dedicated solely to beer-making, or a few minutes spent in the company of a brewing enthusiast, will convince the uninitiated that this is a black art, more at home atop a Gothic tower than in a kitchen. All the brewers I have met are men obsessed (and they have all been men). They talk animatedly and sometimes darkly about unfermentable sugars, degrees Lovibond, EBUs, SRM and the relative merits of CaraMunich Malt III and CaraMunich Malt I.

How much of this esoterica do you need to know to brew beer? Ultimately none at all – all you need to do is follow a recipe. But it is interesting and useful to learn about what is going on, not least so that you know how important it can be to stick closely to a recipe. When the temperature for the mash is given as 66°C the writer *means* 66 degrees and for good reason, and when a particular hop is specified you cannot easily replace it with another; it would be like substituting sprats for haddock in a fish pie.

Of all the home brewing I do, beer-making is the most satisfying. When making beer you feel that you are doing something important, something that makes the world better. How right you are. It is an artisan pursuit and, as someone who has been a furniture maker, I feel completely at home. Beer can be ready very quickly – 3 weeks or even less for some brews – and always much quicker than wines.

Many of the beers that follow use a range of wholegrain techniques, some of which are little used by even the dedicated home brewer, such as using a single mash to produce two or more beers (parti-gyling or split-gyling). I also give several recipes that use malt extracts, which avoid much of the hard work associated with wholegrain brewing.

Krausen or froth after 2 days of fermentation

Malt: the basis of beer

Alcohol, as we know, is produced by yeast acting on sugar (see p.13 for a full explanation). Beer is made from cereals, usually barley, that contain small amounts of sugar but large amounts of starch. A considerable part of the beer-making process is spent converting that unusable starch into yeast-friendly sugar.

When a barley grain absorbs moisture it starts to germinate. This produces enzymes, which begin to convert the starch within the grain to sugars – sugars that are destined to nourish a young plant. If we wanted barley plants we would let nature take its course, but we do not, so the germination process is stopped at a very early stage by heating and drying, effectively killing the grain but leaving the enzymes intact. This leaves the grains with a barely depleted starch content, and with a sufficiency of newly created enzymes to convert this starch into sugar. It is with these dried grains, known as 'malt', that the brewing process truly begins.

Crystal malt

Wholegrain and extract brewing

There are, in effect, two methods of making beer, though they can both be used in a single brew. These are 'wholegrain' in which you start with grains, i.e. malt, and 'extract' in which you start with malt extract – the sugars and the flavours having been industrially extracted from the malt.

Wholegrain For this style of beer-making, you use a process called mashing to convert the starch in malt into sugar, followed by sparging to extract the sugar (see p.180 for more details). This method gives you complete control over the beer you make and I quite like the challenge of big kit and the complicated processes it involves; I feel I deserve the resulting beer a little more. Purists will always opt for wholegrain brewing but you only have yourself to please so do not be pressured, even by me, if you do not wish to take that path.

Extract Extract beers are also derived from malt, but the complicated process of converting the starch to sugar and extracting the sugar has been done for you. With extract brewing your starting point is tins of sticky malt extract or packets of dried malt extract powder.

Malt extract beers miss out the mashing and sparging processes which occupy so much of a brewer's time. They also miss out some of the kit. You will need only those pieces of equipment required for the boil and beyond. This method also allows you to make strong (high gravity) beers more efficiently than in wholegrain brewing, where large quantities of partially used grains either have to be thrown away or employed to make a second, weaker beer. What malt extract beers cannot do is provide you with the full depth of flavours you get when making your own mash, where you can control the types of sugars extracted. It also feels a little bit like cheating, but perhaps that is just me.

Making extract beers saves so much time and hard work that it is the only way many people brew their beer. After mucking about with wholegrain brews for years my father was eventually lured to the dark side. He made hundreds of gallons of beer this way and, being more interested in saving money than finding a way of filling time, never regretted it. Extract brewing is the method you would be using if you bought a beer-making kit; there is nothing wrong with kits – they make excellent beers – they just take a little of the fun out of things.

Some brews use both malts and malt extract, sometimes employing a malt extract as the base malt (providing the bulk of the sugars) and special malt for flavouring and colour – and in the particular case of crystal malt (see p.187), for sugar as well. Malt extracts are also used in addition to grains in wholegrain brewing to increase the strength of a beer.

The method

Here is a general description of the beer-making process. Extract brewing misses out the first two steps (see p.179), which may not seem much of a help but it is. Lager-making follows the procedure up until fermentation, after which the temperatures and timings are quite different.

Mashing Malted barley grains are steeped in hot water, activating the enzymes they contain. These enzymes then convert the starch in the grains into fermentable sugars and some unfermentable sugars. The thin porridge-like mixture is called the mash and the bucket where the magic happens, the mash tun (pic 1, p.182).

The temperature at which the enzymes work best is 66°C, and the conversion process typically takes 1¼ hours. It is very important (it *really* is) to keep the mash at around 66°C using blankets and duvets, because the chemical reaction slows to a crawl if the temperature drops too much.

Straining The sugar solution is filtered from the mash, leaving the grains behind. To do this, the mash is poured into a fermenting vessel which has holes drilled in the bottom and has been lined with a nylon mash bag. This is set on top of a large bucket, into which the sugar solution (wort) runs (pic 2, p.182).

Sparging The amount of wort collected in this way is small and very high in sugar. It is possible to make beer out of it, but not much and it will be very strong. There is still a great deal of sugar in the mashed grains and this needs to be extracted. This, combined with the extra water needed to achieve the extraction, will give a wort with the correct sugar level. The standard method is sparging, where hot water is slowly sprinkled over the grains until the volume of wort required is achieved and most of the sugar extracted. I suggest a variation on this technique which I still call sparging though, technically, it is not: Water is heated in a large pan to about 78°C and, using a plastic jug, carefully poured over the grains in approximately 2-litre batches, flooding the grains. The wort slowly trickles through (it takes about 10 minutes) and the process is repeated until the required amount of wort is collected (pic 3, p.182). The grains are discarded.

Boiling The wort is boiled for about 1½ hours (pic 4, p.182).

Adding the hops and other ingredients to the boil At the beginning of the boil (copper-up), hops are thrown in. Hops added early impart bitterness to the beer; hops added towards the end lend aromatic flavours. Other flavour ingredients and additives such as copper finings can also be added at various stages during the boil.

Standing To extract the flavours the wort is left to stand off the heat for up to 1 hour.

Filtering The used hops and other solid matter are filtered out using a colander and the wort is transferred to a fermenting vessel (pic 5, p.183). The used hops are retained as they will be needed again.

Liquoring down Cold water is added to the wort to make up the volume required and to reach the correct sugar level. The latter is tested by taking small samples, cooling them quickly and using a hydrometer.

The most common method of liquoring down is known as 'cold sparging' – passing cold water through the colander of used hops (pic 6, p.183).

Cooling To avoid cloudiness in the form of a 'protein haze', the wort is cooled rapidly to near room temperature so that any proteins still in solution clump together and fall out of suspension.

Aeration Once the wort is at room temperature (about 20°C) it is aerated vigorously by being splashed about with a hand or electric whisk. This is because yeast needs oxygen for the early stages of vigorous fermentation. Do not aerate the wort while it is hot, as this may cause it to oxidise, forming the off-flavour of wet paper bag.

Pitching Yeast is added to the wort and the lid fitted to the fermenter to prevent contamination. If the lid fits so tightly as to form a perfect seal an air lock should be fitted to allow carbon dioxide to escape.

Fermentation The brew in the fermenting vessel (pic 7, p.183) should be kept at 18–25°C at all times unless otherwise stated in the recipe – lager, for example, requires a lower temperature. The wort is kept covered until fermentation has stopped, with the 'krausen' or brown froth sometimes skimmed off. Fermentation should take about 5 days. Once any remaining froth has sunk to the bottom of the fermenter and the air lock stops bubbling, a hydrometer is used to check the specific gravity of the liquid and determine if fermentation has ended. The specific gravity can vary from beer to beer depending on the level of unfermentable sugars.

Racking and fining What could now arguably be called beer is racked (transferred using a siphon), into a second fermenting bucket if you want to bottle your beer or into a cask (pic 8, p.183) if you don't. This separates it from the lees (dead yeast cells and other debris at the bottom), which would produce off-flavours if left in contact with the beer. Finings, which guarantee a clear beer by precipitating out particles from the liquid, can be added, though to be honest I never bother with them.

Mashing

Straining the mash

Sparging the mash

The boil

Straining out the used hops

Cold sparging the used hops

Fermentation

Racking into cask

Conditioning This is the continuation of fermentation to carbonate the beer (make it a bit fizzy). To start conditioning, a small amount of sugar is added to the beer (priming). This is added to the cask for cask-conditioned beer and to the fermenting vessel for bottle-conditioned beer, the beer being bottled as soon as fermentation becomes evident (bubbles appear). Bottle conditioning can also be achieved by adding ½ tsp sugar to each bottle before filling with the beer but if fermentation refuses to get going again you will have a flat, rather sweet beer.

Maturation The beer is ready after about 10 days for most brews, but strong beers can take much longer.

Nothing to it really. I will fill in even more details with the first recipe, which will be the model for many of the others, and, I hope, make things seem a little less daunting than they might appear at this point.

Variations on the method

There are, of course, endless variations, one of which is brewing lager (see opposite). Others include:

Parti- or split-gyling Sometimes (and I like this one) you can make two or even three different brews from the same mash; the wort that comes straight from the mash and the early part of the sparging contains high levels of sugar and can be used to make a very strong beer. The wort from later sparging will become progressively weaker and can be used to make progressively lighter beers. This technique is used by brewers; if you see Old Bastard 3.8% ABV and Complete Bastard 5.2% ABV pumps next to one another on the bar they probably came from the same mash. It is also possible to blend the different worts to get an almost infinite variation.

Adding hops at different stages Occasionally all of the hops are added at the beginning and in some cases extra hops are put into the beer when it has almost finished fermenting – 'dry-hopping' as it is called.

Underletting In some breweries, hot water is introduced during mashing. There are practical reasons for this, which are not relevant to home brewing, but, by increasing the temperature of the mash, underletting changes the types of sugars extracted from the malt. Because these are often unfermentable sugars, they will not be converted into alcohol and will round the flavour of the beer by sweetening it. The home-brew equivalent is to stir some hot water into the mash after half an hour or so. I have used it in a few recipes because they are adapted from professional brews, though how effective it is on a small scale is debatable.

Lager

Despite an appreciation of the finer points of 'proper' beers I still have an inordinate fondness for lager. People are very sniffy about this fine drink. I remember a visit to the remote North (Derbyshire) many years ago when a request for half of lager in the local pub had me down for the soft southerner that I am. To me, a good lager has a freshness seldom found in other beers, and there is nothing better on a hot day. For the home lager brewer, however, there is a problem. Lager is easy enough to make on an industrial scale but not on the small. It's all down to temperature.

Lager-making is different in several ways from normal beer-making. Instead of pale ale malt, lager malt is used as the base malt and the hops are different, with exotic names such as Hallertau or Saaz. The most important difference is in the yeast, which is a different species called *Saccharomyces pastorianus*. It is a 'bottom-fermenting', rather than a 'top-fermenting' yeast, and acts more slowly, generally settling at the bottom of the fermenting vessel rather than rising with the foam.

Also, and this is critical, lager yeast ferments at lower temperatures, typically 7–15°C. It thus produces fewer of the highly flavoured esters (pear drops, fruity flavours and many more) of the top-fermenting yeasts, which work at temperatures of up to 25°C. The lack of esters provides the clean flavour (or lack of flavour!) that people like about lager. Because the temperatures in lager-brewing are necessarily lower, it takes much longer than normal beer-making. This is what gave the drink its name: 'lager', from the German *lagern*, which means 'to store'.

It is the temperature constraints which make lager a difficult brew to master. The yeast is usually pitched into the wort when the latter is at 20°C or just below. Once the fermentation has got going – normally a few hours after pitching – the wort is moved to a cool area. The temperature should be around 10–12°C. It is left until the fermentation ceases, and then racked off into a fresh container.

Next, a 'diacetyl rest' is performed. The temperature is raised for a couple of days to enable the yeast to remove the diacetyl which accumulates in slow brews. Without this procedure your lager will taste of butter. For more information on this sometimes troublesome chemical, see p.204.

The lager is then conditioned for several weeks at a temperature of approximately 5°C. Strategically situating it in a shed during the winter will often do the trick, especially if you cover the container with blankets to prevent serious day/night swings of temperature. Realistically though, it would have to be a hard winter to maintain such a low temperature for so long. However, your lager will turn out fine provided it is reasonably cold most of the time. By far the most reliable method is to have a fridge dedicated to the task. A standard fridge has a 100-litre capacity and can usually accommodate a suitably shaped 25-litre container. At home I have a wine-cooler which lives in the loft and does the trick nicely.

A selection of commonly used malts

Ingredients

There are very few ingredients in beer but what there are come in a bewildering number of varieties, several of which may make an appearance in a single recipe. Beer recipes often look like incomprehensible shopping lists. The basic ingredients are malt, hops, finings and yeast. A few other things such as different cereals, flavourings, inorganic compounds such as gypsum and salt, and various sugars sometimes find their way into a recipe. As discussed on p.188, malt extract may be used instead of or in addition to malt.

Malt and other grains

The list of malts available is overwhelming. If you take into account varieties and regional variations there are around five hundred. However, they do fall nicely into a dozen or so basic types and, better still, these can be divided into two general categories – base malts and speciality malts.

Base malts (usually pale ale malt or Golden Primrose, though sometimes lager malt) are the basis for most beers and it is perfectly possible to make a beer using just a base malt. They contain starch ready to be converted into sugar and the enzymes ready to do the converting.

Speciality malts may or may not have the enzymes but they will usually, though not always, have at least some starch which in one special case comes ready-converted to sugar. What speciality malts do is to provide their own particular flavours and colours but they are able to rely on the base malt to provide the enzymes which convert their starches if this is needed. Generally a beer will be made mostly with a base malt which is flavoured and coloured with a number (sometimes a large number) of speciality malts.

The different malts are made by varying the malting process, most often the drying temperature. Pale malt, for example, is dried at a relatively low temperature, preserving the enzymes and not toasting it. Amber, brown, chocolate and black are progressively darker malts subjected to progressively higher temperatures. Black malt looks (and tastes) like the stuff you scrape off toast before you can eat it.

Crystal malt, which comes in a variety of shades and sugar profiles, is unusual in that most of the starch has already been converted to sugar, as it is wetted after drying and then dried again when the enzymes have done their job. If the malt is re-dried at a high temperature some of the sugars caramelise and become unfermentable and so retain their sweetness in the finished beer.

Acid malt is an interesting malt, as the lactic acid tang it provides is useful in the making of lager.

If you see the mysterious symbol L° on the label it simply refers to the colour where, for example, 2L° results in a pale ale or lager and 35L° in a stout. The 'L' is a reference to one of the brothers Lovibond who came up with this bright idea; 35L° would therefore be rendered as 'thirty-five degrees Lovibond'.

Other grains Barley is not the only cereal used to make beer. Unmalted wheat, corn, oats and other grains are often added to beers for their special qualities, such as removing protein hazes, reducing tannin levels, improving the head and adding flavours in the form of esters for hints of banana and cloves. The starches in these grains are converted to sugar by the action of the enzymes in malted barley.

Wheat and oats can be malted to make wheat and oat beers, though a base barley malt is usually used to maintain sugar levels and provide extra enzymes.

The point of describing all this is to reassure you that the large number of malts and other cereals called for in some recipes is actually needed; the various malts are very different and they can make very different beers.

Malt extracts

Malt extracts are used instead of or in addition to malts in beer-making. They are the basis of extract brewing, removing the necessity to extract the sugars, colour and flavours from malt grains yourself. All the extraction work has been carried out in a factory and the malt extract supplied in tins or packets ready for use.

They come in a variety of colours (very pale, pale, dark, and so on) and produce different coloured beers. Malt extracts all have individual sugar profiles with varying amounts of unfermentable sugars, which can affect the finished sweetness and body of a beer. These are not usually referenced on the packaging but the information can be obtained from the supplier. Malt extracts can also be used in wholegrain brews to increase the original gravity.

Specific gravity

The amount of malt or malt extract used to make a given volume of beer is the chief determinant of the original gravity (OG) of the beer, the specific gravity just before fermentation is started. Once fermentation is complete the beer will have a final gravity (FG). Using the simple formula (OG—FG) x 0.13 it is easy to roughly calculate the percentage alcohol content of the beer, as the difference between the two gravities indicates how much sugar has been converted to alcohol. With an original gravity of 1042 and a final gravity of 1007, for example, you will have a 4.5% ABV beer. Beers are often spoken of as being high, medium or low gravity, references to their original gravities and likely alcohol content.

Beers with a final gravity above 1010 tend to taste sweet; below this, even though sugars are present, they are barely detectable. Beer never reaches the low final gravity of wine (1000 or less), as it contains high levels of unfermentable sugars.

Malt extract

Hops

Hops

Hops are, relatively speaking, a new invention. Before the arrival of hops, ale was flavoured and preserved with a variety of unlikely herbs. However, the hop's ability to keep ale fresh – and, quite frankly, give it a vastly improved flavour compared to what went before – soon made it a near essential ingredient in ale. Thus it was that ale became beer. But not everyone was pleased. Henry VIII took particular exception to hops and banned them. A long and tedious poem of 1661 by one 'Antidote' and not very wittily entitled The *Ex-Ale-tation of Ale* praises ale in every verse while attacking beer and hops and taking side swipes at Calvinism on the way.

> *And in very deed, the hop's but a weed*
> *Brought over against the law, and here set to sale,*
> *Would the law were renew'd, and no more beer brew'd,*
> *But all men betake them a pot of good ale.*

The hop genus, *Humulus*, has only three members, of which *Humulus lupulus*, the common hop, is by far the most important. The nearest genus to *Humulus* is *Cannabis*, an unsurprising fact if you are familiar with both plants. Indeed the resin that collected on the knives of Kentish hop-pickers was once used as an invigorating addition to tobacco, showing that the plants share more than an ancestor. But such dark thoughts must be put aside; we are only interested in the benign qualities that hops give to beer. If you have never smelled a handful of dried hops you are in for a treat. They are aromatic, heady and crying out to be included in perfumes as a guaranteed attractant to warm-blooded males. They are, after all, flowers.

Three characteristics are supplied by hops: bitterness, complex aromas/flavours and preservatives.

A list of available hops is as long as a list of available malts, making endless permutations possible. Many are grown in Britain – Fuggles and Goldings being the best known – but many more are grown abroad and imported. With hops you often have to give up the idea of food miles, because many recipes call for hops from distant lands. Of course if you want to stick to domestic hops you can; it just slightly restricts the type of beers you can produce.

Hops are almost always used in dried form, sometimes in vacuum-sealed packets, sometimes just in a bag, and occasionally as pellets. They deteriorate quite quickly so if you have some left over, keep them in the freezer.

It is possible to use completely wild hops in your beer, though the flavour will be quite random and they do not provide a great deal of bitterness. However, if you do find some, they can be used in a once-a-year brew that is much looked forward to in many hop-growing areas. Although I have never used the wild hop flowers for beer, I collect young hop shoots in the spring. They are rather good in a stir-fry or an omelette.

Bittering hops The bitterness in a beer comes from alpha acids in the hops that are added at the beginning of the boil – the bittering hops (see p.180). Such hops do not need to be particularly fragrant, because any fragrance would be lost during boiling anyway. The alpha acids, which are present in surprisingly large – if variable – quantities in hops, are, unhelpfully, insoluble in water. The boiling process, however, turns them into soluble 'isomers'. If you are interested, an isomer of a compound is a rearrangement of its constituent atoms in a new shape: in this case the boiling reorders the molecular structure of the alpha acids into molecules that *are* soluble in water. It takes around 45 minutes for the isomers to be created. Boiling for a shorter length of time just wastes alpha acids as they will not become soluble and a longer boil will only slightly increase the bitterness.

If you look at a catalogue of hops you will find a description of each hop that includes the bitterness that can be expected from it. This is expressed as the percentage of alpha acids, which can range from 3% to nearly 20%. The final bitterness of a beer depends on four things – the quantity of hops used, the percentage of alpha acids in the hops, the boil-time and the original gravity (the level of sugar in the wort).

The higher the original gravity, the less bitter the beer will be because sugar reduces the solubility of the alpha acids. In short, strong beers need more alpha acids than weak beers to reach the same level of bitterness. The technical term for this is 'hop utilisation'.

The final bitterness of a beer is expressed in IBUs (International Bitterness Units). If you think all this is complicated then I tend to agree with you. However, you only need to worry about such matters if you are inventing your own recipes and all the recipes here have been invented (and tried!) already.

Finishing hops If the bitterness of hops and the sometimes toasty qualities of malts were the only flavours in beer it would be a dull drink. Many of the fine aromas and flavours we expect come, unsurprisingly, from aroma hops. They are also known as 'finishing hops' as they 'finish' the beer.

Although some hops have both good bittering qualities and good aroma qualities, there are many specialised finishing hops that contain small quantities of highly aromatic essential oils. These are very volatile and would be lost if added at the beginning of a long boil so they are added towards the end. Just 15 minutes before 'heat off' is typical, with more added 10 minutes later, though this can vary from recipe to recipe. Sometimes the hops are added just as the wort comes off the heat, 'at knockout', and sometimes they are added to the cask after fermentation has more or less ceased – 'dry-hopping'.

Each one of these methods will produce different flavours, as each has a different effect on the amount of essential oils that are released and then retained.

Brewers hate to waste anything so it is common practice to 'cold sparge' the hops and other solid matter that was filtered out earlier with cold water, running it into the wort (see p.181). This extracts the last bit of flavour from the hops and also rescues a considerable amount of wort.

Yeast

Although most of the yeasts used in brewing are *Saccharomyces cerevisiae*, brewer's or baker's yeast, this species comes in a large number of varieties. Their primary task is to convert water and sugars into alcohol, but they are also responsible for many of the subtler flavours found in beers. As with malts and hops, each variety of yeast produces its own characteristic flavour – though some are more neutral.

Different yeast strains also act differently during the fermentation process. They may possess talents, such as the ability to sink conveniently to the bottom of the fermenter once they have finished their work, or tolerate low temperatures or high alcohol levels.

For us home brewers, yeast is most likely obtained in dried form in little packets sufficient, usually, for a 25-litre batch. You can also buy them in impressive little test tubes, though these are usually the more specialist home-brew yeasts which come with fancy names such as 'Brew Lab 2000 Somerset 1'.

As with wine-making, wild yeasts floating around in the air sometimes get into a brew; in fact some beers, called 'lambic beers', rely entirely on wild yeasts. Lambic beers are a little worrying because, while they often work out well with some unusual but pleasant flavours, sometimes they don't, and 25 litres is a lot of beer to empty down the drain.

Flavourings

Although hops, malt and the activity of yeast produce most of the flavour of beer there is no real reason why you cannot add any flavour that takes your fancy. Most flavourings are added towards the end of the boil to ensure that they have time to find their way into the wort, but not so much time that the flavours boil away.

The recipe on p.207 uses orange as a flavouring and most other fruits will have an interesting effect on the taste of the finished beer; one must simply be confident that it is a pleasant effect too. Traditional ale flavourings such as burdock or sweet gale can also be used to give a taste of ancient brews, and I have included recipes that do just that on pp.236 and 238.

Commercial breweries sometimes add unusual ingredients towards the end of fermentation as I discovered on a visit to the St Austell Brewery in Cornwall, where I saw a huddle of brewers frantically cutting off the green bits from 500 kilos of strawberries for a special strawberry-finished lager. They sent me a few bottles later and the effort seemed entirely worthwhile.

Finings

One utilitarian addition to a wort or beer is finings. These natural materials clarify the beer by collecting the cloudy particles and precipitating them to the bottom of the fermenter. They come in two varieties: copper finings and beer finings.

Copper finings A favourite copper fining is the common seaweed carragheen. This is something I collect and dry myself and I like the idea that I have foraged at least a tiny part of my beer. Carragheen is easy to find on rocky shores but also easy to buy if you are not near the seaside. Carragheen is a copper fining because it is put in the boiling pot, traditionally called the 'copper', not because it is some nasty compound of copper. It is also available in tablet form under the name Protofloc.

Beer finings Copper finings only help precipitate out the proteins; to clear the beer of dead yeast, beer finings can be added to the fermented beer prior to conditioning. Strangely, many of these too have a maritime origin, being made from boiled crustaceans. You can usually get away without using beer finings because most beers clear with time, and many real-ale fans consider the obsession with crystal-clear beers to be a passing fad. Certainly they are not needed in dark beers.

Sugar

The most important use of sugar in brewing is to extend the fermentation process once the main flush of yeast activity has passed. This extra sugar (usually plain sucrose) is added to the bottles, fermenter or cask to condition the beer. The yeast will release a predictable amount of carbon dioxide, giving the beer a bit of fizz and head. Adding sugar in this way is called priming.

Sugar is also occasionally added to a boil with the sole intention of making the beer a little stronger without using extra malt which might make the flavour too heavy because of its distinctive taste and unfermentable sugars. Invert sugar – a mixture of glucose and fructose derived from the more complex sucrose – is often used, as is glucose (sometimes referred to as 'brewing sugar') alone.

Seemingly contrary to this, sugar can be added during the boil to sweeten a beer, giving it more body. There would be no point in using ordinary white sugar for this as it would be consumed by the yeast, but many dark sugars contain unfermentable sugars that the yeast cannot devour. Very dark raw sugars and caramel contain sufficient quantities of these to sweeten a beer with the bonus of adding colour.

Brewing salts

Various inorganic compounds such as gypsum, bicarbonate of soda and calcium carbonate are often added during the boil to adjust the pH of the water used and to improve the 'mouth-feel' of the finished beer.

Dried carragheen

My 72-litre copper

Equipment

If you wish to use the traditional method of wholegrain brewing that I champion, you do need a lot of 'kit', and big kit at that. With wine you are dealing with just a gallon or maybe two, but home-brewed beer can only sensibly be made in 25-litre (5-gallon) batches. I do, however, make many test batches of only 10 litres, and if you want to make beer on this very small scale you will find that the equipment is much more manageable. All of the items below can be obtained from home-brew suppliers. Malt-extract brewing calls for fewer fermenting buckets and you will not require a mash bag. All the equipment assumes a batch size of around 25 litres.

Copper For the domestic situation only a stockpot will be large enough for this job. It must be capable of holding at least 30 litres of liquid and come with a lid. I always like my kit big, but slightly regret buying the 72-litre stainless steel monster that now lives in the garden because it will not fit in the shed, let alone the kitchen.

A copper is also used to heat the water for the mash and the water for sparging. You will, of course, need a hob to heat it up on.

Thermometer This is absolutely essential in beer-making, as the brewing process is very temperature-sensitive. A plain glass thermometer is best.

Weighing scales These need to be capable of accurately weighing anything from 10 kilos (malts) to just a few grams (hops and other light ingredients).

2-litre plastic measuring jug You will need a jug to pour water for sparging and for other tasks.

Long-handled plastic spoon Used to stir the mash and the boil. A plastic spoon is easier to keep sterile than a wooden spoon.

Fermenting buckets Although called fermenting buckets, these are used for all sorts of things. They are made of food-grade plastic. Two of the buckets require some very low-tech modifications and they all need lids. The following list may seem like a lot of buckets but it does make things much easier:

- A 25-litre bucket in which to make your mash (although it is possible to use a smaller bucket for small mashes).

- A graduated bucket with a capacity greater than 25 litres to collect the wort. Now 25-litre fermenting buckets are often slightly larger than 25 litres, whatever

Beer fermenting vessels

The modified fermenting vessels

they may call themselves, and this is the sort that you need. Most have volume markings on the side and if there seem to be 2 or 3 litres beyond the 25-litre mark that is the bucket for you. Failing this, a 33-litre bucket will be fine. Whichever size you use the lid must be flat (not domed in any way). Cut a circular hole in the lid, which leaves about 4cm of polythene around the inside of the rim. This is so that you can sit the next bucket to be described on top and allow the wort to flow through.

- A 25-litre bucket identical to the previous bucket. This one holds the grains while they are being sparged. You will need to drill about forty 3mm holes in the bottom as it is going to act as a very large sieve into which the mash is poured from the mash bucket.

- A 33-litre bucket for fermentation. The extra 8 litres are to accommodate the froth that rises to the top of a brew. The lid should have a single hole in it to accommodate a rubber grommet for an air lock.

Mash bag This is a large nylon bag which is used to contain the mashed malted barley inside the poor fermenting bucket that has the holes drilled in it.

Colander Sieving out the hops and other solid matter is best achieved with a deep colander lined with muslin.

Muslin cloth Used to line the colander (above) and to make 'hop bags' for dry-hopping. The bag of hops is tied with string, leaving a long piece to suspend the bag in the cask or fermenter. When the lid is screwed on it will stay in place.

Cooling equipment The wort needs to be cooled rapidly after the boil and some method must be devised for doing this. Acquiring new kit is, however, optional because you can simply stand the fermenting bucket, full of hot wort, in a large sink of cold water and throw in some ice. My preferred method involves a large flexible builder's bucket partially filled with water and, again, ice.

A much more efficient, sophisticated and downright complicated approach is to buy some 10mm copper pipe and some fittings and make a helix that fits into your 33-litre fermenting bucket – a 'cooling coil'. Using a hosepipe, cold tap water is run through the helix until the temperature of the wort is reduced. I will leave the fine details of this up to you.

Whisk An electric or hand whisk is used to aerate the wort.

Siphon tubes These come as simple flexible plastic tubes which can be adorned with rigid plastic tubes, a little device on one end to preventing sucking up the lees, or with clips to attach it to a fermenting bucket. You can also buy self-priming siphons which save a great deal of sucking and mess.

Hydrometer An essential item, this measures the specific gravity of a brew. Calibrated to work at 20°C, a hydrometer will give a misleading reading if used at higher or lower temperatures. A small quantity of wort or beer should be transferred to a trial glass and cooled before testing. For more on hydrometers, see p.15.

Trial glass To hold a sample of beer or wort for testing with a hydrometer.

Heating equipment Maintaining a steady temperature for your brew can be very difficult. The ideal temperature for most fermentations is 20°C, or up to 25°C for a fruity beer, and it is best if the temperature is kept at the same level. If you have a room that maintains this temperature day and night it will be fine. Otherwise buy a flexible builder's bucket large enough for your 33-litre fermenting bucket to fit inside and a thermostatically controlled 150-watt waterproof aquarium heater. The fermenting bucket is placed inside and water poured around it until it just starts to float. Suspend or otherwise fix the heater, set to 20°C, in the water at about the halfway mark and plug it into the mains.

Incidentally, with 25-litre batches it is seldom necessary to cool your beer, though the heat of fermentation itself can require cooling in commercial breweries. If your brew threatens to go beyond 25°C, drape wet towels over the fermenting bucket. This Heath Robinson arrangement works very well but is a bit messy.

Barrels or casks These come in 10- and 25-litre sizes. They are fitted with a tap and a screw top with a very simple pressure valve in the middle. In fact it is just a collar around a small spigot with a hole in the side. It will maintain a pressure just a little above atmospheric. I prefer to keep my beer in cask (the effort of removing bottle caps has become too much for me) and I have accumulated a large and proud collection.

If you want to bottle your beer you can keep it in a cask to settle and mature first or you can use the fermenting vessel below.

25-litre wide-neck fermenting vessel A 25-litre wide-neck fermenting vessel is useful if you wish to bottle your beer. Some come with a tap fitted – or you can fit one yourself. Although it is possible to bottle beer using a siphon it is tricky and inevitably messy; a tap makes things much easier, especially when fitted with a bottle-filling attachment.

Bottle-filling attachment This is a tube, long enough to reach the bottom of a beer bottle; on the end is a valve so that when you take the bottle away the flow will stop. I love these things as they take the stress out of bottling and prevent most of the sticky floor problem that has caused so much domestic exchange over the years.

Beer bottles These can be bought new but it is an ideal opportunity to recycle. Beer bottles are easily obtainable from pubs, because breweries seldom want their bottles back these days. For advice on how to deal with recycled bottles, see p.17. Alternatively, you can buy swing-top bottles.

Bottle or 'crown' caps These come in a range of colours, presumably so you can colour-code your beer collection. They come in bags of one hundred.

Crown capper There are several gadgets designed to fit crown caps to beer bottles. I use a simple hand-held device, which must be hit nerve-wrackingly hard with a hammer. A bench-mounted capper is a more sedate option, though more expensive.

Carbonator This is optional but I would never be without one. It is a sad fact that as you draw beer from a cask the amount of beer left in the cask is reduced. This is hard enough to bear, but after a pint or two the pressure of the carbon dioxide in the cask (which was produced by the conditioning process) is also reduced and the beer no longer flows unless you allow air in by loosening the screw top. Oxygen and beer do not make happy companions and the beer can quickly go sour. Letting air in can also introduce micro-organisms which will also make the beer sour.

A simple, cheap solution to these problems is to fit a carbon dioxide cylinder to the barrel, replacing the plain plastic screw cap with a valved plastic screw cap that will receive a carbon dioxide cylinder. Once the gas is turned on, the headspace is then filled with carbon dioxide, pressure is restored and the beer will flow again. This is not quite the same as adding carbon dioxide to a beer – that would need a great deal more kit and carbon dioxide than can easily be provided at home. But the beer comes out with a good, or at least big, head and you can taste the extra fizz.

Two simple arrangements are possible – disposable carbon dioxide bulbs and reusable carbon dioxide cylinders. Fitting either of these is scary the first time you try it because there is a great deal of fizzing and the cask inflates as though it is about to take out both you and the kitchen. Do read the instructions on the side of the reusable cylinders; take the advice on only giving one-second bursts seriously.

If you want to impress absolutely everyone however, a pressure-regulated system complete with dials, valves and pipes is available to buy surprisingly cheaply.

None of the above items of equipment are hard to obtain or particularly expensive.

Cleanliness

It is worth mentioning that half of the disasters that beset the early days of my beer-making career were due to inattention to timings or attempting to ferment at the wrong temperature, and the other half to a lack of scrupulous cleanliness.

You do not need to worry about your equipment being sterile until the moment you turn the wort off the boil – you could use a stockpot with traces of last week's vegetable stew in it or throw in old socks; it would not affect the brewing process at all, though it would not help the flavour particularly. But as soon as the gas goes out you must be very careful; everything that the wort or beer touches after that must be sterile. The cleaning process is described on p.16.

The wort should always be kept covered in the fermenting vessel until it is ready to bottle or keg, though you are allowed to take an occasional peek and sniff to check everything is going to plan. You have already aerated your wort so exposing it to further air will not help and may introduce unwanted livestock such as fruit flies. Once fermentation has ceased the beer should be handled carefully and not splashed around too much as this will introduce oxygen when it is not wanted.

Keeping records

Record-keeping is a major part of brewing and some of the old record books kept by ancient brewers make fascinating reading. For example they often give the weather on brew days going back centuries – a resource for historical climate data buffs. You do not need to note that it is a fine sunny day but it is really important to record everything else. The recipe itself must be recorded or referenced of course, along with timings, specific gravities, temperatures and pH if you have a meter. You should also keep comprehensive records of the appearance and taste of your brew at strategic moments in its life.

Such records help enormously if things go wrong and enable you to tweak the recipe or your method if you think of possible improvements. While most people are happy to produce elderberry wine without resorting to pen and paper, beer-making is sufficiently complicated to merit extremely careful records.

Things that go wrong with beer

There are a lot of these – but I expect you guessed that already. However, you should not run into any problems provided you stick to the correct temperatures and timings, and keep everything covered and very, very clean.

Contamination by malicious bugs is the cause of most beer disasters. This is a *good* thing because cleanliness is actually very easy to maintain, and such problems are correspondingly easy to avoid. See p.202 for my cleaning recommendations.

If there does not appear to be anything much wrong with your beer apart from the fact that it doesn't taste very nice I advise you to give it time. We seldom expect wines to be drinkable within a week or two and this can apply to beers as well. I have lost track of the number of occasions I have found a beer to be disappointing only to revisit it 3 months later to discover it has matured to glory. So be patient, and do not consign a brew to the sink until all hope is lost.

Assuming you avoid all or most of the problems associated with bacterial or fungal contamination, what other disasters lie in wait?

Buttery taste to the beer

This extraordinary 'problem' is down to a chemical called diacetyl which makes things taste buttery. You take a sip of beer, everything seems to be fine, then your mouth fills with the taste of butter. In small quantities it improves the flavour of many beers, giving them a rounder taste. But in some it is a disaster; lager makers in particular go to great lengths to remove as much diacetyl as possible.

Diacetyl is a natural product of the brewing process and it's quite likely that the buttery flavour will become pronounced at some point during beer-making. Fortunately it is absorbed by live yeast and is likely to disappear altogether without any intervention.

Incomplete fermentation, however, often results in excess diacetyl so the following steps are particularly important in bringing the levels down:

- Ensure there has been adequate aeration before adding the yeast.
- Pitch enough yeast to give your brew a good start.
- Do not shock the beer with wildly varying temperatures during fermentation.
- Low fermentation temperatures can raise diacetyl levels, so keep to the suggested temperature.
- Ensure good hygiene to avoid infection, which can also result in diacetyl.

If you still find that your beer is too buttery (usually this will be evident when you rack it) then raise the temperature a little to stimulate the yeast for 2 or 3 days. This is called a 'diacetyl rest' and it is standard practice in many breweries. This rest can sometimes be encouraged by adding 2 tbsp sugar to keep the yeast active; it may even help to add some high-powered 'restarter yeast' to get things going.

Do not worry too much – several times I have thought of chucking a batch of beer down the sink only to find that a week later it tasted just fine. There was evidently enough yeast activity to remove the diacetyl.

Off-flavours

The most common cause of off-flavour is autolysis, the breakdown of the dead yeast cells that accumulate in the bottom of your fermenter. Once it starts it can quickly ensure that your beer tastes of wet dog or cheese long past its sell-by date. Fortunately it takes a fair amount of neglect for this unpleasantness to occur, and racking off a day or two later than anticipated is unlikely to cause any problems.

There are many other off-flavours available to the careless or unlucky brewer, most of which are down to poor hygiene or, at least, very bad luck – a vinegar fly diving into your fermenting bucket during the few seconds it is uncovered, for example. Overheating the wort during fermentation and exposing the wort or finished beer to sunlight can also produce unpleasant flavours and aromas. The answer to the last two is don't.

Stuck fermentation

I hate this. Such joyous hopes travel with our brews and to see them sulking on Tuesday when they seemed so happy on Monday feels like a betrayal. Prevention really is better than cure here. If your fermentation is stuck then something was not right from the beginning.

If your beer does not ferment at all (no bubbles, no smell of carbon dioxide, nothing) then there is probably something wrong with your yeast and you should re-pitch with fresh yeast. This is a very rare occurrence and I cannot remember the last time I encountered a bad yeast.

If the fermenting temperature is correct and you aerated your wort thoroughly then a stuck fermentation is unlikely. The first step is to check if you really do have a stuck fermentation – it may be just a completed fermentation. Test the specific gravity, and if it is much higher than the final gravity that you are anticipating then the fermentation is indeed stuck.

Once you've established that you have a stuck fermentation check the temperature. If it is not correct then move the fermenter to a more salubrious environment. It is worth stirring the wort to swirl any live yeast that may have settled to the bottom back to the top where it will do some good. Adding a fresh batch of yeast may also help. Special 'restarter' yeasts, which can tolerate being introduced to a partially brewed beer, are available. There's even a type of yeast selected for use at the priming stage – when stuck fermentation is particularly common, resulting in a flat beer.

Most yeasts can be sprinkled on, but if this fails, then mix a little warm water with 1 tsp sugar and the yeast in a jug. Cover and leave until fermentation is well under way then add about 50ml of the stuck beer. Wait until this starts fermenting then add another 100ml beer. Once this is fizzing away merrily pour it back into the fermenter and keep your fingers crossed. If all is well you should see signs of fermentation within an hour or two.

Simple model brew:
Orange pale ale

ORIGINAL GRAVITY	1040–1042	4.3–4.5%
FINAL GRAVITY	1007	ABV

This is among the simplest wholegrain beers I know and it is very reliable. The brewing process itself is as straightforward as things can be in a wholegrain brew. If you are new to beer-making I strongly suggest you try this brew first, or at least read the recipe carefully as it gives an essential introduction to the basic process of wholegrain brewing. I have divided the stages to make what will still seem like a horribly complicated process a little less forbidding.

Each of the subsequent brews will follow, more or less, the same basic process. Temperatures, quantities, timings, ingredients and occasionally parts of the method will vary, but once you know how to make this brew you will understand how to make the rest. Even malt-extract brewing follows the same process except that it leaves out the first two steps, replacing them with the adding of malt extract at the start of the boil.

Orange beer is one of the three beers that I do not like to find myself without, so I make a batch every few months. It uses only a base malt – English pale ale malt – and a single hop – East Kent Golding, an all-round hop which is mildly bittering (4–5.5% alpha acids) and has flowery finishing qualities. The finished beer is very light with a nice top note from the orange peel. The orange can be left out if desired and other flavourings added – two (gloved) handfuls of nettles will give you a nettle finished beer, a sliced 3–5cm piece of ginger root will give you a ginger beer, and so on. Among the best of the variations is spruce beer. Gather the young, pale green tips in spring and early summer and add a small handful instead of the orange peel.

As with all beers, temperatures are critical, so do keep to them as closely as you can. There is a great deal of logistical manoeuvring with liquids being poured from one container to another so keep calm. As this is a model brew I will go through all the stages in detail. This and all the other beer recipes are for about 25 litres.

The specific gravities you actually get may vary from those provided – it all depends on how efficient your mashing and sparging are. Don't worry about this unless it is a long way out. If it is more than three or four points too low then either add some malt extract before the boil or, since the wort becomes a little more concentrated during the boil, you can make a little less beer instead. In this case miss out or reduce the liquoring down. The only potential issue with this is that if you are leaving it in the cask it will have an air gap at the top, though since this is usually filled with carbon dioxide it is seldom a problem. If your specific gravity is too high then you will just get a stronger and sweeter (full-bodied) beer.

Makes about 25 litres

4kg pale ale malt
30g East Kent Golding hops
200g brown sugar
Zest of 1 unwaxed orange

2 tsp dried carragheen
11g sachet ale yeast
1 tsp beer finings
50g sugar for priming

Mashing Place the malt into a fermenting bucket. Your humble fermenting bucket has now been promoted to a 'mash tun'. It is important to make sure that the malt is at about room temperature before you begin the mash. Heat 13 litres water in your copper to 76°C. Pour and stir the hot water into the malt to make your mash, which should end up at close to 66°C; this temperature is called the 'mash heat'. You can safely tweak it by stirring in hot or cold water. Fit the lid. The temperature should be maintained for 1¼ hours, so stand the fermenting bucket on something insulating and cover closely with blankets or a duvet.

Sparging While your mash tun is doing its bit, heat about 17 litres water to 78°C in your stockpot. It will need to be kept at this temperature throughout this process, which calls for constant checking with thermometers and adjusting hob knobs.

Now a bit of kit preparation. Fit the lid with the very large hole cut out of the centre onto the 25-litre fermenting bucket *without* holes in the bottom. Stand the fermenting bucket *with* the holes in the bottom on top of the other bucket, with its bottom resting on the lid. Drape the mash bag inside the top bucket and tie in place with the string provided. It is worth putting the handle of a teaspoon between the bottom of the top bucket and the lid of the bottom bucket to release air, which can force the wort all over the floor.

When the mash is ready, carefully pour all of it into the top bucket. The wort will run through to the bottom bucket. Wait until most of it has gone through then use a plastic jug to carefully pour 2 or 3 litres hot water over the surface of the malt until it floods a little. Wait until the wort almost stops running out of the bottom then sprinkle on another 2 or 3 litres water. Continue until you have almost 25 litres wort in the bottom bucket. About another 1 litre wort is available to make up the 25 litres by lifting and gently squeezing the mash bag. Do take your time with the whole sparging process – at least an hour – so that as much of the sugar is collected as possible. You can, if you want, use the practice of slowly sprinkling the hot water onto the mash but it is boring and will not produce better results. The grains are no longer required for your brew (but chickens love them).

It is well worth testing the wort with a hydrometer at this point. The specific gravity of a cooled sample at this stage should be about 1041. What do you do if it isn't? A higher specific gravity does not matter but if it is below 1036 stir in some pale malt extract, 50g at a time, until 1041 is reached. You may like to drink a little of your wort at this point; it tastes like watery Horlicks.

The boil Pour the wort into your copper. I suggest using your plastic jug to transfer at least half of it as a 25-litre bucket full of hot wort is a little unwieldy. Bring the wort to the boil and add 10g of the hops and all of the brown sugar; this is called adding ingredients at 'copper-up' – the moment when the wort comes to the boil.

Boil the wort gently for a *total* of 1¼ hours with the lid on, adding another 10g hops, the orange zest and carragheen after 1 hour, and stirring in the third and final 10g hops after 1 hour and 10 minutes.

Standing Turn off the heat and leave the copper to stand for 40 minutes. From this point onward *everything* that touches the wort or beer needs to be sterile.

Filtering Pour the wort into the 33-litre fermenting vessel through your muslin-lined colander. Stand the colander of soggy hops in a clean bowl for use later.

Liquoring down Add cold tap water (most tap water will be near enough to being sterile) to the wort by passing it through the colander full of used hops (cold-sparging), until a specific gravity of about 1040–1042 is reached. This is the original gravity. The cold sparging returns some sugars and flavours to the wort. If you checked and perhaps adjusted the specific gravity at the end of the sparge there should be about 25–26 litres. Do not worry unless it's wildly out; once, when it was I got away with adding malt extract at this point to give the correct SG and volume.

Cooling Cool rapidly by standing the bucket in a sink or flexible builder's bucket full of water and then adding ice to the water, or use a cooling coil (see p.199). Leave it to cool to about 20°C.

Pitching the yeast Aerate the wort by whisking or stirring with a large whisk to ensure that it has enough oxygen to allow your yeast to grow. Pitch the yeast and cover with a lid that has an air lock fitted. Keep at 18–25°C (20°C is ideal), checking to make sure a nice foam has formed after a day. After about 5 days this foam will sink to the bottom as the fermentation slows or stops. Check the specific gravity at this point; it should be about 1007.

Racking The beer needs time to mature and clear, and also needs to be removed from the layer of dead yeast at the bottom of the fermenting vessel. If it is not then autolysis (decomposition of the dead yeast) can occur and produce off-flavours.

Separating the beer from the lees is done by 'racking off' into a cask or wide-neck fermenting vessel using a siphon. Do not splash the beer to allow in oxygen.

Finings Stir in the finings after 3–4 days, using your long-handled spoon. This is strictly optional as the beer will likely clear anyway.

Conditioning and storing After 7–10 days, prime the beer by stirring 50g sugar into the cask for 'cask-conditioned' or into the fermenter for 'bottle-conditioned'. It is worth leaving the sugar for a day or so in the fermenter before bottling to see if fermentation has started again (you should see bubbles rise from the surface of the beer). If it sits and does nothing for 2 days, restart the fermentation as for a stuck fermentation by making a restarter batch as described on p.205. The sugar does not have to be added to the fermenter; instead you can place ½ tsp in each bottle before adding the beer, but it is impossible to fix things if refermentation refuses to start.

The beer is ready to drink after 2 weeks. In bottle-conditioned beers you will find a sediment forms at the bottom of the bottle; this is as it should be – just pour carefully. Sediment will also form in the bottom of a barrel but, being below the tap, is usually no trouble.

Ordinary bitter

ORIGINAL GRAVITY	1039	4.2% ABV
FINAL GRAVITY	1007	

If whisky is the national drink of Scotland then bitter must be the national drink of England. No pub will be without a bitter and many boast several from a number of different brewers. Apart from the brewer's name on the pump they are identified as 'ordinary', 'best' and 'special', reflecting their alcohol content. 'Ordinary' will be around 4%, 'best' around 4.5% and 'special' anything stronger. I have called this 'ordinary' only in this technical sense; it is one of the best bitters I have tried.

It could be argued that 'bitter' does not actually taste all that bitter. The term was invented by pub clientele to distinguish it from mild ale, which was, well, mild; the brewers just used to call it light bitter ale, or pale ale, if it was stronger. This bitter contains some wheat malt, which improves the 'head' and 'mouth-feel'.

Makes about 25 litres

4.5kg pale malt
200g wheat malt
350g crystal malt
50g chocolate malt
25g Pacific Gem hops

2 tsp dried carragheen
25g East Kent Golding hops
11g sachet ale yeast
1 tsp beer finings
50g sugar for priming

Place the malts in a fermenting bucket, mix well and stir in 14 litres water at 75°C. The mash heat should be 65°C. Cover and keep it warm for 1¼ hours.

Sparge as normal with water at 78°C until you have 25 litres wort.

Pour the wort into your copper and boil for a total of 1½ hours, adding the Pacific Gem hops at copper-up and the carragheen and East Kent Golding hops 15 minutes from the end. Allow to stand for 40 minutes.

Transfer to your fermenting bucket, straining out the used hops, liquor down until the specific gravity is at 1039, then cool rapidly.

Aerate and pitch the yeast at 20°C. Leave to ferment for about 5 days until fermentation is complete and the specific gravity is about 1007.

Rack, fine and prime as usual, depending on whether the brew is to be bottled or left in cask. Most bitters are left in cask so I should stick with tradition.

Special bitter ale

ORIGINAL GRAVITY	1051	5.2% ABV
FINAL GRAVITY	1012	

Back in 1902, S.W. Arnold of Taunton made a Special Bitter Ale using Oregon hops. To make a beer which is similarly spicy and fruity, I am using Bramling Cross hops which, although English, have the flavour of the old American hop. The original recipe also calls for both Chilean and Smyrna pale malt, food miles evidently not being much of a concern back then; I'm bringing these ingredients closer to home too.

Makes about 25 litres

2.2kg English pale ale malt
2.2kg Scottish Golden Promise malt
500g flaked maize
4 tsp gypsum
75g East Kent Golding hops
200g Mauritian light brown sugar
200g invert sugar

2 tsp salt
2 tsp dried carragheen
45g Bramling Cross hops
11g sachet English ale yeast
1 tsp beer finings
50g sugar for priming

Put the malts and maize into a fermenting bucket. Heat 14 litres water to 74°C, add half the gypsum, then stir into the malts and maize. The mash heat should be 67°C. Cover and keep warm for 1¼ hours.

Sparge with water at 78°C until you have 25 litres wort.

Pour the wort into your copper. Boil for a total of 1 hour 50 minutes, adding 30g of the East Kent Golding hops, the brown and invert sugar, the salt and the rest of the gypsum at copper-up. The carragheen is added at 1½ hours and the Bramling Cross hops 10 minutes later. Leave to stand for half an hour, then strain into a fermenter.

Liquor down until you have a specific gravity of 1051. Cool rapidly.

Aerate and pitch the yeast when the wort is at around 20°C. Leave to ferment for about 5 days until fermentation is complete and the specific gravity is about 1012.

Rack into a barrel or wide-neck fermenter and add the rest of the East Kent Golding hops tied in a muslin bag. Rumble the barrel or fermenter every day for a week or two to distribute the hop flavour around the beer.

After 2 weeks it may be fined and primed in the barrel or bottled in the usual way.

Alastair's session bitter

ORIGINAL GRAVITY	1038	
FINAL GRAVITY	1011	3.8% ABV

I know few people who talk as much as my friend Alastair and none who talk so much about beer. He devised this award-winning beer for his old brewery in Wiltshire and it's one of his favourites. Even people who do not really like beer tell me they love its lightness and hoppy flavour and I have to tell them to stop drinking mine and make their own. A 'session bitter' is any beer between 3 and 4% ABV which has a good balance of hops and bitterness and no particularly strong flavours that might become tiresome after more than five pints. In other words, one that's good for a 'session'.

Makes about 25 litres

3.5kg English pale ale malt
75g crystal malt
100g amber malt
40g Whitbread Golding Variety hops,
    blended with 25g Fuggles hops
4 tsp gypsum

1 tsp cooking salt
2 tsp dried carragheen
11g sachet English ale yeast
15g Fuggles hops (for dry-hopping)
50g sugar for priming

Place the malts in a fermenting vessel and stir in 7.5 litres water heated to 75°C. The mash heat should be 64°C. Cover and maintain this temperature for 40 minutes, then stir in 3 litres water at 76°C. Cover and keep warm for a further 50 minutes.

Sparge with water at 78°C until you have 25 litres wort.

Pour the wort into your copper and boil for a total of 1¾ hours. Add 50g of the Whitbread Golding and Fuggles hop blend, the gypsum and salt at copper-up and the remaining hop blend and carragheen at 1½ hours. Let stand for half an hour.

Transfer to your fermenting bucket, straining out the used hops, liquor down until the specific gravity is at 1038, then cool rapidly.

At 20°C aerate and then pitch the yeast. Leave for about 5 days until fermentation is complete and the specific gravity is about 1011.

Rack into a barrel or wide-neck fermenting vessel with the Fuggles dry-hopping hops in a bag. Leave for 2 weeks, rumbling every now and then.

Prime as usual, depending on whether the brew is to be bottled or left in cask.

Aleister Crowley's AK bitter

ORIGINAL GRAVITY	1031	
FINAL GRAVITY	1007	3.1% ABV

This rather weak, low-hopped beer would probably be described as a 'mild' these days, but Crowley & Co. called it a 'bitter' so we shall stick with that. It may come as a surprise that this odd and notorious occultist – once called 'the most evil man that ever lived' – had anything to do with brewing and, truth be told, he didn't. Crowley & Co. was sold in 1879 and Aleister lived on the inheritance so derived. The origin of 'AK' has been the subject of much speculation but one explanation is that it is an abbreviation of *ankel koyt*, a type of pale beer from northern Germany.

Makes about 25 litres

3kg English pale ale malt
250g crystal malt
60g East Kent Golding hops
350g Edme SFX dark malt extract
(or similar)

10g gypsum
2 tsp dried carragheen
11g sachet English ale yeast
50g sugar for priming

Place the malts in a fermenting vessel and stir in 7 litres water heated to 73°C. The mash heat should be 63°C. Cover and keep warm for half an hour.

Stir in 2.5 litres water at 82°C. Cover and keep warm for another hour.

Sparge with water at 75°C until you have 25 litres wort. Transfer to your copper.

Boil for a total of 1½ hours. Add 35g hops, the malt extract and gypsum at copper-up then another 15g hops and the carragheen after 1 hour. Let stand for half an hour.

Pour into a fermenting vessel, straining out the used hops, then liquor down until the wort reaches a specific gravity of 1031. Cool quickly.

Aerate, and then pitch the yeast at about 20°C. Leave to ferment for about 5 days, skimming after 2 days, and again after another day.

Once the beer reaches a specific gravity of 1007, rack into a barrel or wide-neck fermenting vessel, adding the remaining 10g hops in a muslin bag. Leave for at least 3 weeks, rumbling the barrel or fermenter every now and then.

Prime as usual, depending on whether the brew is to be bottled or left in cask.

Strong East India pale ale

ORIGINAL GRAVITY	1066	6.8% ABV
FINAL GRAVITY	1014	

It began with a problem. The British of the Raj, like the British everywhere else, liked their tipples. Beer was the solace of choice for most of them but beer is not easily brewed in the subcontinent, at least not until fairly recently. Madeira was consumed by the boatload, but there is only so much Madeira you can drink, and palm sugar wine and its distilled offspring, arrack, were consumed in vast quantities to provide variety and economy. However, they were deadly brews, notoriously, on one occasion, claiming the lives of several Englishmen during a single evening bash. A less troublesome replacement was needed.

Unfortunately, beer does not travel well over such distances and certainly not at the temperatures it encounters while travelling them; it almost invariably went bad. Several solutions were suggested, such as making a concentrated wort, shipping that and adding water and yeast when it arrived – a sort of beer 'pot noodle'. It did not work well.

The answer was simply to make a beer that kept well. Enter Mr Hodgson of Bow Brewery in East London. Two things stop beer having the shelf life of milk: alcohol and hops. Mr Hodgson's simple solution was to increase both – a lot. His India pale ale used heroic quantities of malt and hops, with extra hops added to the finished beer just in case. He also primed the beer with a greater than usual amount of sugar so that the barrels gently fizzed all the way to India; a live beer is unlikely to go sour.

Modern IPAs are, for the most part, poor imitations of Mr Hodgson's original brew and most are really just bitters. The alcohol content is usually a paltry 4.5% and a journey to the Isle of Wight can be touch and go. However, you can pickle a dog in this 6.8% beer.

The recipe is taken from a brew made in Swanage, Dorset, at the height of British influence in India. It has a back-breaking malt bill and a wallet-threatening hop bill, but it is a truly remarkable beer. It is extremely aromatic because of the high level and varieties of alcohols and esters it produces, and thick enough to stand a spoon in upright (though only a metal spoon; plastic ones dissolve).

Finally, there is the delightful bonus of my Small beer (see p.219), which must be made very soon after, or even at the same time as, the IPA. You will be very busy juggling pots and buckets so try to keep focused and don't plan to do anything else that day.

Be warned, this is strong stuff and the higher alcohol content makes it almost immediately soporific. Fortunately it has never given me a hangover as I have always fallen asleep after one pint.

Makes about 25 litres

9.5kg English pale ale malt	2 tsp dried carragheen
1kg crystal malt	2 x 11.5g sachets high-alcohol yeast,
4 tsp gypsum	such as Safbrew S-33
190g East Kent Golding hops	50g sugar for priming

Put the malts in a large fermenting bucket; you will probably need to employ your 33-litre bucket for this. Heat 21 litres water to 74°C and mix with the malts in the bucket. The mash heat should be 64°C. Cover and keep warm for 1½ hours.

Sparge with water at 78°C until you get 25 litres wort. Now if you also wish to make the recipe on p.219 (and you really should, otherwise the leftover sugar-rich mash is wasted) you have to start it at this point!

Pour the wort into your copper. Boil for 1¾ hours, adding the gypsum and 90g of the hops at copper-up, another 90g hops after 1 hour and the carragheen after 1 hour 20 minutes. Allow to stand for half an hour.

Pour into a fermenting vessel, sieving out the used hops, then liquor down until the wort reaches a specific gravity of about 1066. Cool quickly.

When it is at room temperature pitch both sachets of yeast – you need an extra dose because yeast can struggle to get going at high sugar concentrations. Cover and leave to ferment for about 5 days. After 2 days skim off the foam and do this again the next day.

Once it reaches a specific gravity of 1014, rack the beer into a barrel or wide-necked fermenting vessel, adding the remaining 10g hops tied in a muslin bag. Give the hops a month to infuse the beer, rumbling for the first 2 weeks.

Prime with sugar as usual, depending on whether you intend to bottle or keep your beer in cask. Either way, this beer benefits enormously from being left to mature for a few months. Drink with extreme caution.

Small beer

ORIGINAL GRAVITY	1035	3.7% ABV
FINAL GRAVITY	1007	

This beer follows on from the IPA on p.216 and it is frankly not that small. It uses 'parti-gyling', which is not something you hear much of these days. Most recipes make an 'entire' beer; i.e. malt is used to make a single beer and then thrown away. Parti-gyling is where you make a strong beer from the first sparging of the malt and a weaker beer from the second sparging; sometimes a third beer is made, and this is a 'small beer'. These three beers can be blended, providing yet more variation.

But three spargings is a lot to ask from the home brewer so we shall content ourselves with two. When you make your IPA you should be prepared with extra 25- and 33-litre fermenting vessels because this beer must be made the same day.

The partially used malt left over from the IPA should be *still hot and where you left it* in the mash bag and fermenting bucket-cum-colander.

Makes about 25 litres

Malt left over from the IPA (on p.216)   **11g sachet English ale yeast**
60g East Kent Golding hops   **1 tsp beer finings**
2 tsp dried carragheen   **50g sugar for priming**

Heat 25 litres water to 78°C. Place a fresh fermenting bucket under the bucket/sieve containing the partially sparged malt and sparge with the hot water until the specific gravity of the wort is down to 1035. You will need to test quite often to avoid over-diluting it. How much wort you will get depends on many factors; you may not get 25 litres in which case adjust the amount of hops accordingly.

Pour the wort into your copper. Boil for a total of 1¼ hours, adding 20g of the hops at copper-up, another 20g hops and the carragheen at 1 hour, and the final 20g hops 5 minutes from the end. Allow to stand for 40 minutes.

Transfer to your fermenting bucket, straining out the used hops, liquor down until the specific gravity is at 1035, then cool rapidly.

Aerate and pitch the yeast at 20°C. Leave to ferment for about 5 days until fermentation is complete and the specific gravity is about 1007.

Rack into a barrel or fermenter, then continue with finings and sugar as usual, depending whether you want a cask-conditioned or bottle-conditioned beer.

John Wright & Sons
Experimental India beer

ORIGINAL GRAVITY	1050–1054	4.7–5.2%
FINAL GRAVITY	1014	ABV

Since I have only daughters you can be assured that the John Wright in question is another fellow altogether. He was in fact a Scot whose company brewed from the early nineteenth century in Perth, Scotland. It is his company, not he, that is responsible for this beer, since he died in 1849, over fifty years before it was brewed.

This is an unusual beer because it contains no hops – an ale in the strictest sense. It is also known as gruit, an old name for a herbal, unhopped beer. Hops were expensive in early twentieth-century Scotland so it is unsurprising that they were optional. Scotland's most famous drink, whisky, is at heart a distilled, unhopped beer.

If you think this beer will have little flavour, a quick look at the list of ingredients will both reassure and worry. The moment all these unlikely compounds are added to the copper an encouraging and unexpected hoppy smell arises.

Everything here is highly flavoured, especially the wormwood, which is also slightly poisonous, though not in the tiny quantity used. (It is however best avoided if you suffer from epilepsy, or if you are an expectant or nursing mother – you can easily replace it with twice as much mugwort.) The original recipe called for gunpowder. Quite what that is doing in a beer is a mystery solved by assuming it is a reference to 'gunpowder tea', something I found in a box of mixed teas given to me one Christmas by someone who obviously didn't like me very much. All I remember about it is that the leaves were enormous and the taste nothing like that of tea.

If you want to use more foraged ingredients for this recipe, I suggest hogweed seeds or flower heads to replace the cardamom pods.

Makes about 25 litres

4.5kg Golden Promise malt
700g crystal malt
700g coarse rolled oats
25g gypsum
15g dried yarrow
   (preferably in flower)
7g dried rosemary
   (preferably in flower)

7g cardamom pods or 15 hogweed
   seeds or 3 hogweed flower heads
4g dried wormwood or 8g mugwort
25g green gunpowder tea
2 tsp dried carragheen
2 x 11g sachets English ale yeast
1 tsp beer finings
50g sugar for priming

Put the malts and oats into your fermenting bucket. Heat 10 litres water to 80°C and stir into the malt and oat mix. The mash heat should be 67°C. Fit the lid and keep warm for 1½ hours.

Sparge with water at 78°C until you have 25 litres wort.

Pour the wort into your copper. Boil for a total of 2 hours, adding the gypsum, yarrow, rosemary, cardamom pods, wormwood or mugwort and gunpowder tea at copper-up, and the carragheen 10 minutes from the end. Leave to stand for 40 minutes.

Transfer to your fermenting bucket, straining out the used flavourings, then liquor down until the specific gravity is between 1050 and 1054. Cool rapidly.

At around 20°C, aerate then pitch the yeast. Leave to ferment for about 5 days.

Rack into a barrel when fermentation is complete and the specific gravity is down to about 1014. Fine and prime as usual, depending on whether the beer is bottled or kept in cask. I strongly suggest leaving this in the cask as it benefits greatly from long maturation.

Black pearl porter

ORIGINAL GRAVITY	1042	
FINAL GRAVITY	1007	4.5% ABV

This brew is from my friend Mark Jenkin of the Mighty Hop Brewery down the road in Lyme Regis. To be precise, the brewery is situated in the shed at the end of Mark's garden and boasts an impressive array of gleaming stainless-steel cylinders, pipes and gadgets. Mark is the sort of enthusiast I love, making first-class brews with a passionate intensity. I haven't asked why it is called Black pearl porter but no doubt he is a fan of pirate movies. Please note that the instructions below should be strictly adhered to – they are rules, not guidelines!

Makes about 25 litres

4.7kg pale malt
700g crystal malt
150g chocolate malt
15g Green Bullet hops
2 tbsp golden syrup

15g East Kent Golding hops
2 tsp dried carragheen
11g sachet ale yeast
50g sugar for priming

Combine the malts in a fermenting bucket and stir in 15 litres water at 76°C. The mash heat should be 66–67°C. Cover and maintain this temperature for 1¼ hours.

Sparge with water at 78°C until you have 25 litres wort.

Pour the wort into your copper. Boil for a total of 1½ hours, adding the Green Bullet hops at copper-up and the golden syrup, East Kent Golding hops and carragheen 15 minutes from the end. Allow to stand for 40 minutes.

Transfer to your fermenting bucket, straining out the used hops, then liquor down until the specific gravity is at 1042. Cool rapidly.

At about 20°C, aerate then pitch the yeast. Leave to ferment for about 5 days until the fermentation is complete and the specific gravity is about 1007.

Rack and prime as usual, depending on whether the brew is to be bottled or left in cask.

Stout

ORIGINAL GRAVITY	1046	
FINAL GRAVITY	1013	4.3% ABV

This beer is strong, and as black as night. It is an unusual beer in that it contains liquorice. It was made by Kidd & Company in Dartford during the First World War and I like to imagine it was the beer my grandfather drank with a steak and kidney pie (he called it the best meal he ever ate) on his return to London from the trenches.

A mere 3g may not seem like much liquorice but this tar-like 'juice' is strong stuff. It was, and still is, called liquorice juice even though it's sold in pellet form. If you can't find it you could use a couple of real liquorice twigs from a wholefood shop instead.

Makes about 25 litres

4kg English pale ale malt
500g brown malt
500g crystal malt
300g black malt
20g salt
3g liquorice juice
500g Edme SFX dark malt extract
   (or similar)

500g invert sugar
250g liquid caramel
50g Fuggles hops
40g East Kent Golding hops
2 tsp dried carragheen
11g sachet ale yeast
50g sugar for priming

Mix the malts in a fermenting bucket. Heat 7.5 litres water to 79°C and mix with the malt grains. The mash heat should be 65°C. Cover and keep warm for 1½ hours.

Sparge with water at 75°C until you have 25 litres wort.

Transfer to your copper. Boil for a total of 2½ hours, adding the salt, liquorice, malt extract, invert sugar, caramel and 40g of the Fuggles hops at copper-up, the Golding hops at 1½ hours and the carragheen and remaining 10g Fuggles hops at 2 hours. Leave to stand for half an hour.

Transfer to your fermenting bucket, straining out the used hops, then liquor down to 1046. Cool rapidly.

At around 20°C, aerate then pitch the yeast. Leave to ferment for about 5 days, until fermentation is complete and the specific gravity is about 1013.

Rack and prime as usual, for cask or bottle conditioning.

Oat malt stout

ORIGINAL GRAVITY	1050	
FINAL GRAVITY	1015	4.5% ABV

This brew is a brown stout, as opposed to the more familiar black stout on p.223; it is a rich amber colour. Stouts are so called because of their 'mouth-feel' – something everyone who has tried the most famous of all stouts, Guinness, will understand. Fairly ancient recipes for brown stouts abound; one from the *Gentleman's Magazine* of 1768 called for nothing more than brown malt, hops, water and yeast, though you would need to get a grip on bushels and hogsheads. The 1919 beer is light in flavour and has a creamy head, courtesy of the oat malt.

Makes about 25 litres

2.7kg English pale ale malt
1kg oat malt
1kg high-colour crystal malt
800g chocolate malt
500g dark malt extract, such as
    Muntons Dark Spraymalt
65g Fuggles hops

4 tsp gypsum
2 tsp salt
2 tsp dried carragheen
11g sachet English ale yeast
12g East Kent Golding hops
50g sugar for priming

Mix the malt grains in a fermenting bucket and stir in 15 litres water at 75°C. The mash heat should be 67°C. Cover and keep warm for 2 hours.

Sparge with water at 77°C until you have 25 litres wort. Transfer to your copper.

Boil for a total of 1½ hours, adding the malt extract, 25g of the Fuggles hops, the gypsum and salt at copper-up, the rest of the Fuggles hops at 45 minutes and the carragheen at 1¼ hours. Leave to stand for 40 minutes.

Transfer to your fermenting bucket, straining out the used hops. Liquor down until the specific gravity is at 1050, then cool rapidly.

Aerate and then pitch the yeast at 20°C. Leave to ferment for about 5 days until fermentation is complete and the specific gravity is around 1015.

Rack into a barrel or wide-neck fermenter and add the Golding hops in a muslin bag. Rumble the barrel every day for 3 weeks.

Prime and continue as usual for a cask beer or bottled beer.

Puffed wheat beer

ORIGINAL GRAVITY	1040	4.2% ABV
FINAL GRAVITY	1007	

This is not as mad as it sounds. Although barley is by far the most important cereal for beer-making, other cereals are used too, including wheat. Sugar Puffs come ready stocked with fermentable sugars, including 3% honey, and there is plenty of sugar locked into the starch of the puffed wheat grains.

Puffed wheat is also known as torrified wheat and is available from brew shops. It is also added to some commercial beers. What it lacks is the enzymes needed to convert the starch to sugar. For this we use malted barley in the form of pale ale malt, which has enough enzymes to convert its own starch and that of the wheat.

The result is a light beer, with a clean toasty, hoppy taste and it puts a whole new slant on the idea of breakfast. Scale down the recipe to your requirements.

Makes about 25 litres

3kg pale ale malt
1.6kg sugar-coated puffed wheat cereal
200g brown sugar
30g East Kent Golding hops

11g sachet ale yeast
1 tsp beer finings
50g sugar for priming

Mix the malt and cereal in a fermenting bucket and stir in 13 litres water at 76°C. The mash temperature should be 67°C. Cover and keep warm for 1¼ hours.

Sparge with water at 78°C until you have 25 litres wort.

Pour into your copper. Boil for a total of 1¼ hours, adding the brown sugar and 10g of the hops at copper-up, another 10g hops at 1 hour and the remaining 10g hops 5 minutes before the end. Leave to stand for 40 minutes.

Transfer to your fermenting bucket, straining out the used hops. Liquor down until the specific gravity is at 1040, then cool rapidly.

At around 20°C, aerate and then pitch the yeast. Cover and leave to ferment for about 5 days until fermentation is complete and the specific gravity is about 1007.

Rack into a cask or wide-neck fermenter and then leave for 4 days.

Fine, prime and continue as usual for a cask or bottled beer.

Mark's Dorset Pilsner

ORIGINAL GRAVITY	1047	
FINAL GRAVITY	1012	4.6% ABV

I have my friend Mark Jenkin to thank for this ingenious way around the difficulties of lager-brewing. It is simply an ale that uses lager ingredients. It lacks the heaviness of many beers and has the distinctive tang of a lager. I love it and hope that even the seasoned bitter drinker will like it too.

The lager malt is supplemented by another four malts in small quantities – crystal malt for colour, Munich malt for authenticity, acid malt for the 'tang' it provides and Carapils for the unconvincing reason that it allows us to call the beer a Pils. The recipe uses an ale yeast rather than a lager yeast, which saves endless temperature-control troubles but it means that this is not really a lager – it just tastes like one.

Makes about 25 litres

4.5kg lager malt
100g Carapils malt
75g crystal malt
150g Munich malt
75g acid malt
50g Saaz hops

2 tsp dried carragheen
7g Nelson Sauvin hops
11g sachet Nottingham ale yeast
1 tsp beer finings
50g sugar for priming

Mix the malts in a fermenting bucket and stir in 15 litres water at 75°C. The mash heat should be about 66°C. Cover and keep warm for 1¼ hours.

Sparge with water at 78°C until you have 25 litres wort.

Pour the wort into your copper. Boil for a total of 1¼ hours, adding 25g of the Saaz hops at copper-up, the rest of the Saaz hops and the carragheen after 1 hour, and the Nelson Sauvin hops 5 minutes from the end. Leave to stand for 40 minutes.

Transfer to your fermenting bucket, straining out the used hops. Liquor down until the specific gravity is at 1047, then cool rapidly.

At around 20°C, aerate and then pitch the yeast. Leave to ferment for about 5 days until fermentation is complete and the specific gravity is about 1012.

Rack into a cask or wide-necked fermenter and leave to rest for a week.

Fine, prime and continue as usual for a cask or bottled beer.

Rauchbier

ORIGINAL GRAVITY	1055	5.2–5.6%
FINAL GRAVITY	1012–1015	ABV

On a bitterly cold December lunchtime, I visited the Square and Compass in Worth Matravers, Dorset, with my friend and beer guru Alastair. This is a pub without a bar and there are hardly any tables but it has a log fire you could roast a wild boar in, a charm beyond any pub I have ever encountered – and a vast selection of beer.

We thumbed our way through the beer menu and selected a few bottles that looked interesting. One of them was Rauchbier, a German smoked malt beer, which hails from Marzen and Bamberg. It was dark ruby in colour with a slight sweetness and faint taste of smoke, but there was nothing heavy about it and it was not overburdened with hoppy esters. It was, in fact, a lager.

We are used to pale lagers but dark lagers exist too. The best known is Dunkelbier but there are others, Rauchbier among them. Rauchbier simply means smoked beer. At one time all beers were smoked by default because the malts were dried over an open flame from wood or charcoal. The invention of coke allowed for the drying of malt to be smoke-free and pale malts were available for the first time as temperatures could be controlled more easily. Unlike the smoked malts of the whisky distillers, Rauchbier malt has no phenolic qualities, it just tastes a little smoky.

Makes about 25 litres

2.7kg lager malt
1.5kg smoked malt
1.5kg Munich malt
700g CaraMunich malt

50g Hallertau or Saaz hops
2 tsp dried carragheen
1 sachet Oktoberfest lager yeast
50g sugar for priming

Mix the malts in a fermenting bucket and stir in 14 litres water at 77°C. The mash heat should be 67°C. Cover and keep warm for half an hour.

Now add 2.5 litres water at 80°C. Stir, then re-cover and wrap to maintain the temperature. Leave to stand for a further hour.

Sparge with water at 78°C until you have 25 litres wort.

Transfer the wort to your copper. Boil for a total of 1½ hours, adding the hops at copper-up and the carragheen 15 minutes from the end. Leave to stand for 40 minutes.

Transfer the wort to your fermenting bucket, straining out the used hops. Liquor down until the specific gravity is at 1055, then cool rapidly.

At around 20°C, aerate and then pitch the yeast. It should start fermenting within 5–15 hours. Once fermentation has started, place your bucket in a cool place such as a shed or a fridge dedicated to the task; it needs to be at around 10–12°C. Leave to ferment for about 10 days, skimming the froth from the top every now and then.

Rack into a barrel or wide-necked fermenting vessel when the specific gravity has dropped to 1012–1015 and move the brew to a warmer location (20°C) to get the fermentation going again. This is called a 'diacetyl rest' when the yeast removes the diacetyl produced during a low-temperature fermentation. Leave for 3–4 days.

Now move the brew to a cold place – ideally around 5°C.

After 6 weeks, prime and leave in cask or bottle.

Northern mild ale

ORIGINAL GRAVITY	1035	3.7% ABV
FINAL GRAVITY	1005	

Before making this I had only tried mild ale two or three times. And I did not like it much. In my younger days I did proudly tell my father that I had at least made the effort to drink something that wasn't lager but he was unimpressed. That was over thirty years ago and mild ales were very much out of fashion.

Quite what a mild ale actually is has changed over the years. Originally it was an immature beer, later a weak beer and sometimes even just a mildly hopped beer. This recipe comes from the heyday of mild ale in the mid-twentieth century and it was brewed in Manchester. It is unusually dark and has a relatively large amount of hops; it qualifies as mild ale because it is weak – a 'boy's mild'. It tastes a great deal stronger than it is and has a pleasant toasty flavour.

Makes about 25 litres

500g crystal malt
100g black patent malt
1.5kg standard dried malt extract
1kg dark dried malt extract
65g Fuggles hops

75g liquid caramel
2 tsp dried carragheen
11g sachet Nottingham yeast
1 tsp beer finings
50g sugar for priming

Put the malt grains into a fermenting bucket and stir in 15 litres water at 65°C. Cover and keep warm for 40 minutes.

Strain the wort into your copper, removing the grains. Add 10 litres hot water and bring to the boil. Stir in the malt extracts, 40g of the Fuggles hops and the caramel and boil for 1 hour. Add the remaining hops and the carragheen and boil for another 30 minutes. Leave to rest for a further 30 minutes.

Strain the wort into a fermenting bucket. Liquor down to a specific gravity of 1035, then cool rapidly.

Aerate and pitch the yeast at room temperature. Leave to ferment for about 5 days until fermentation is complete and the specific gravity is about 1005.

Rack into a barrel or wide-necked fermenting vessel.

Fine and prime as usual for a cask- or bottle-conditioned beer.

A modern stout

ORIGINAL GRAVITY	1044	4.2 % ABV
FINAL GRAVITY	1012	

This fairly simple brew has one unusual ingredient: roasted barley. It is not to be confused with roasted malt because the barley was never malted. Roasted barley gives a dark colour to the beer without the bitterness of black malt; it also gives a creamier head. I have suggested a rather fancy yeast but any English ale yeast would be fine. This beer requires a 'mini-mash' at the beginning but this is not too onerous a task.

Makes about 25 litres

150g crushed roasted barley
150g pale malt
500g high-colour crystal malt
500g chocolate malt
2.7kg dark dried malt extract
250g invert sugar
250g Mauritian unrefined brown sugar

30g Challenger hops
40g East Kent Golding hops
2 tsp dried carragheen
15g Fuggles hops
WLP002 English ale yeast tube
50g sugar for priming

Put the roasted barley and pale malt grains into a bowl and pour on 1 litre water heated to 78°C. Cover and leave to steep for 1 hour.

Put the remaining grains in a fermenting bucket, add the 'mini-mash' and stir in 14 litres water at 65°C. Cover and leave to stand for 1 hour.

Strain the wort into your copper and add 10 litres water. Bring to the boil, adding the malt extract, sugars and Challenger hops at copper-up. Boil for a total of 1¾ hours, adding 25g of the Golding hops and the carragheen 15 minutes from the end. Turn off the heat and stir in the Fuggles hops. Leave to rest for half an hour.

Transfer to your fermenting bucket, straining out the used hops. Liquor down until the specific gravity is at 1044, then cool rapidly.

Aerate and then pitch the yeast at 20°C. Cover and leave to ferment for about 5 days until fermentation is complete and the specific gravity is about 1012.

Rack into a barrel or wide-necked fermenting vessel, adding the remaining 15g Golding hops in a muslin bag. Mature for a couple of weeks.

Prime and continue as usual for cask- or bottle-conditioned beer.

India pale ale

ORIGINAL GRAVITY	1050	5.0% ABV
FINAL GRAVITY	1012	

For anyone who finds the Strong East India pale ale on p.216 too much of a good thing, this will come as light relief. It is much easier to make of course, because it is entirely an extract brew, requiring no grains at all, but it is also considerably weaker, coming out at around 5%, which enables you to drink more than a pint without passing out. It also lacks the powerful esters and is much more like the IPA you get when you ask for one in the pub.

Makes about 25 litres

2.7kg dark malt extract
1.2kg light dried malt extract
80g Styrian Golding hops or Fuggles
    hops, plus an optional extra 15g

2 tsp dried carragheen
11g sachet English ale yeast
1 tsp beer finings
50g sugar for priming

Bring 25 litres water to the boil in your copper and add the malt extracts and 40g of the hops. Boil for a total of 1¾ hours, adding another 20g hops and the carragheen after 1½ hours and another 20g hops when you turn the heat off. Leave to stand for 40 minutes.

Transfer to your fermenting bucket, straining out the used hops. Liquor down until the specific gravity is at 1050, then cool rapidly.

Aerate and then pitch the yeast at 20°C. Cover and leave to ferment for about 5 days until fermentation is complete and the specific gravity is around 1012.

When fermentation is completed, rack into a cask or wide-necked fermentation vessel. You may also add an extra 15g hops in a muslin bag to the cask if you want it 'hoppier'. Leave to mature for a couple of weeks.

Fine, prime and continue as usual for a cask- or bottle-conditioned beer.

Mephisto lager

ORIGINAL GRAVITY	1041	
FINAL GRAVITY	1005	5.0% ABV

Most species of beer can be made with malt extract, and lager is certainly not an exception. This is a pretty standard pub lager and none the worse for it. Like all lagers it is the devil to make, hence the name, but at least the list of ingredients is reassuringly short and there is no messing about with grains. I suggest extra pale malt extract but use lager malt extract if you can find some. Lager-making in general is discussed on p.185.

Makes about 25 litres

3kg spray-dried extra pale malt extract
20g Saaz hops
20g Styrian Golding hops
20g Hallertau hops

2 tsp dried carragheen
2 x 11g sachets Czech Pilsner yeast
1 tsp beer finings
50g sugar for priming

Bring 25 litres water to the boil in your copper and stir in the malt extract. Add the Saaz, Styrian Golding and 10g of the Hallertau hops at copper-up. Boil for 1 hour 20 minutes, then add the carragheen and boil for a further 20 minutes. Turn off the heat and stir in the rest of the Hallertau hops. Leave to stand for 40 minutes.

Transfer to your fermenting bucket, straining out the used hops. Liquor down until the specific gravity reaches 1041, then cool rapidly.

Aerate and then pitch the yeast at a low room temperature (about 17°C). Cover and leave until the fermentation has begun, then move the fermenter to a place that can be maintained at a fairly constant 10°C. If the area is subject to fluctuations in temperature then wrap the fermenter in several blankets once it has reached the required 10°C. Or use a fridge. Leave to ferment for 2 weeks until the specific gravity is around 1005.

Rack into a cask or second fermenter. Move to a warmer area (about 20°C) and leave for 3 or 4 days; this will remove the diacetyl.

Now move the cask or fermenter back to a cooler environment (below 10°C) and leave to mature for a further 12 weeks, adding finings towards the end of this time.

Rack again into a cask, prime and either leave in the cask or bottle.

Heather and honey ale

ORIGINAL GRAVITY	1042	4.0% ABV
FINAL GRAVITY	1010	

This highly modernised version of an ancient beer is mostly grain-free and the wild ingredients are relatively easy to find if you have access to the countryside. Common heather or ling can be found throughout the country except for a broadish band running from Bristol to the Wash. Bell heather is an alternative. Yarrow is a roadside and pastureland plant found everywhere. Sweet gale, also known as bog myrtle, occurs commonly in, you guessed it, bogs and generally damp acid soils. You can replace sweet gale with East Kent Golding hops if you prefer a more beery taste.

Makes about 25 litres

500g crushed crystal malt
1.5kg Edme SFX light malt extract (or similar)
125g heather tips (the softer green parts of the plant, with flowers if possible)
30g dry heather twigs (to provide tannin)

60g yarrow (the feathery leaves plus the flowers if possible)
30g dried sweet gale
2 tsp dried carragheen
1.8kg honey (ideally heather, but cheap honey will be absolutely fine)
11g sachet ale yeast
50g sugar for priming

Put the crystal malt grains in a fermenting bucket and stir in 10 litres water at 65°C. Cover and leave to steep for 40 minutes.

Strain the wort through a muslin-lined colander into your copper. Add 5 litres hot water to the wort and bring to the boil. Add the malt extract, heather tips and twigs, yarrow and sweet gale and boil for 1 hour. Savour the truly wonderful aroma. Add the carragheen and honey and boil for another 30 minutes, then leave to rest for a further 30 minutes.

Transfer to your fermenting bucket, straining out the used flavourings. Liquor down with 10–12 litres cold water until you have about 26 litres wort. The specific gravity should be around 1042.

Aerate and then pitch the yeast at 20°C. Leave to ferment for about 4 days, until fermentation has ceased and the specific gravity has dropped to 1010.

Rack into a cask, prime and continue as usual for cask- or bottle-conditioned beer.

Dandelion and burdock beer

ORIGINAL GRAVITY	1040	
FINAL GRAVITY	1010	4% ABV

One of the unlooked-for joys passed down to us by our ever-busy legislature is the clause in the 1981 Wildlife and Countryside Act which makes it an offence to uproot any plant from the land without the permission of the landowner. Quite what dire problem this piece of legal meddling was designed to solve I do not know, since the removal of rare plants is already prohibited in the previous clause of the same 1981 Act; and why, one wonders, would anyone wish to uproot daisies, three-veined sandworts or grass anyway?

Dandelions, fortunately, are found in almost every garden so they will not be too much of a problem on this front. Burdock is more a plant of the roadside and rough pasture. If you do not wish to endure an uncomfortable conversation with a magistrate and happen to know a sheep farmer (I know about twenty of them, but realise that not everyone is so blessed) the answer is to offer to rid their land of this wool-ruining weed for a small fee.

Dandelion and burdock roots, being perennial, are available all year, but it is important to collect them only when the leaves are visible so that you do not confuse them with anything nasty. Spring or autumn when the roots are at their fattest is the best time to search them out. Burdock has large, heart-shaped, furry leaves and a habit of providing us with those tiresome burs that accompany us home after a country walk.

A circular bulb-planter is the neatest way of uprooting dandelion, but burdock roots are tough, go down a long way in several directions at once and are particularly fond of soil rich in immovable rocks. You will need a spade and a pickaxe. If you are intent on an illicit roadside burdock raid, carrying this equipment in a public place can count as 'going equipped' and could involve free accommodation for up to seven years if things turn out really badly. Foraging can be a nightmare.

While Dandelion and burdock beer is reputed to have a long pedigree going back to St Thomas Aquinas, the earliest reference I can find, beyond a recipe or two, is an 1897 report from Ashton-under-Lyne of some poor devil being fined a couple of quid for selling the stuff. No peace for the enterprising in those days either, it seems.

A variation can be made from another forageable plant: Alexanders. The Latin name of this plant is *Smyrnium olusatrum* (black-rooted thing from Smyrna), which gives a hint that the root is notable, and that it is, indeed, black. Alexanders is a very common seaside plant, particularly fond of coastal roadsides, car parks

and lay-bys. Again it is illegal to dig it up without permission but it is possible to take a few Alexanders seeds from a wild plant and grow them like the related and similarly biennial parsnip in your garden. The flavour is extraordinarily aromatic but lost with prolonged boiling, so for this variation I suggest reducing the boil to just 10 minutes.

Makes 4.5 litres

A couple of large burdock roots
 (about 150g)
A handful of dandelion roots
 (about 50g)
1 tsp dried carragheen

500g sugar
2 tbsp black treacle
Juice of 1 lemon
11g sachet ale yeast

Scrub and finely slice the burdock and dandelion roots. Put them in a large pan, pour on 2.5 litres boiling water and add the carragheen. Boil for half an hour; experience the aroma of an unpromising vegetable stew.

Take off the heat, add 2 litres cold water, the sugar, treacle and lemon juice and stir until the sugar has dissolved. Strain the liquid into a clean fermenting bucket, cover and leave to cool.

When your brew reaches room temperature, pitch the yeast. Cover and leave to ferment for up to a week, until the specific gravity is down to 1010. If you want to be safe, carefully siphon into strong swing-top bottles at this point.

The flavour of dandelion and burdock seems to follow a bell curve of: too sweet, horrible, really rather nice, horrible, poisonous – with the 'quite nice' occurring at the 3–4 week point and extendable by keeping it in the fridge. The flavour is mildly bitter and pleasantly aromatic.

Nettle beer

ORIGINAL GRAVITY	1040	4% ABV
FINAL GRAVITY	1010	

I use nettles a lot. I have made nettle pasta, nettle pakoras and, best of all, nettle soup. A nettle beer can be made using a variation of the model beer recipe on p.207, finishing with a large handful of nettles instead of orange peel. But this is a nettle beer with none of that mucking about with malts and hops – nettleade perhaps. It is a simple, unsophisticated drink, but it reaches all parts quickly and dangerously.

Nettle hunting can be a painful experience unless you go equipped. Thick clothing, rubber gloves and good footwear are essential, but the blasted things will always get you somewhere. Despite extensive precautions, one once managed to go straight up my trouser-leg. I am thinking of buying a bee-keeper's outfit.

Nettles first appear in early spring and this is the best time to pick, though new growth often occurs from cut-down nettle patches. Only pick the young leaves, before the dangling flower heads appear.

Makes 4.5 litres

1kg nettle tops (approximately 1 carrier-bag full)
50g cream of tartar
1 tsp dried carragheen

450g sugar
Juice of 2 lemon
11g sachet ale yeast

Bring 5 litres water to the boil in a large pan, add the nettle tops, cream of tartar and carragheen and boil for about 15 minutes, stirring from time to time. Strain the liquor through a colander or sieve into a fermenting bucket. Add the sugar and stir until dissolved. Leave to cool to room temperature.

Add the lemon juice and the yeast. Cover and leave to ferment for 3 days – this will probably do the trick but if you want to be safe, bottle when it reaches a specific gravity of 1010. Carefully siphon into strong sterilised swing-top bottles, making sure you do not disturb the sediment that will have accumulated at the bottom of the bucket.

The beer will continue to ferment, gradually building up a head of steam, and is ready to drink in a week, although if you leave it longer it will be better. This beer is usually a little cloudy – remember that it is a home brew, so murkiness is considered to be 'character'.

Ginger beer

ORIGINAL GRAVITY	1045	
FINAL GRAVITY	Not applicable	2–3% ABV

'Real' ginger beer is produced by the ginger beer plant, a creamy jelly-like substance which is a complex mixture of yeasts and bacteria – not a plant. The yeast and the bacterium have a symbiotic relationship. The yeast excretes alcohol and the bacteria consume it, allowing the yeast, which can tolerate only low alcohol concentrations, to continue to thrive. Sadly the GBP has suffered a decline and is often difficult to find these days, though you can sometimes source them online.

As with many home brews, it is fascinating to watch the fermentation process, though this mildly alcoholic drink is not to everyone's taste. You will end up with more GBP than you started with but I am sure you will be able to give some away!

Makes 2 litres

5–7cm piece of root ginger, peeled and grated
250g sugar
Juice of 1 lemon
½ tsp cream of tartar

2 litres chlorine-free water (add a large pinch of ascorbic acid i.e. vitamin C or the juice of 1 lemon to remove the chlorine if you are unsure)
About 1 tbsp ginger beer plant (GBP)

The ginger beer plant is a pretty resilient creature but it is safest to make sure everything is clean in the kitchen. Tie the grated ginger in a small piece of muslin. Place it with the sugar, lemon juice, cream of tartar and water in a large jug. Stir until the sugar has dissolved. Add the GBP. Cover with a cloth and fix in place with an elastic band, or just a lid if there is one.

Leave to ferment for about 5 days (or until it tastes just a little sweeter than you would like the finished product to be), then carefully pour into plastic swing-top bottles using a fine sieve or muslin cloth and a funnel. You will find a larger GBP in the sieve than you started with.

Remove the muslin and rinse the GBP in fresh water; use it to make another batch. Your ginger beer will be ready to drink within 2 or 3 days, though it will be fizzier after a week. The low activity of the yeast and small amount of sugar used means that explosive levels of carbon dioxide are not reached, but it is worth checking a test bottle every now and then by loosening the lid just to be sure. Chilling will stop any further fermentation if you are happy with the fizz and sweetness.

Useful Things

Directory

High street shops specialising in items for home brewing are pretty rare these days but online suppliers abound. Most have a large range of equipment and ingredients for all types of home brewing available by mail order.

General suppliers

Dorset Homebrew
www.dorsethomebrew.co.uk

The Home Brew Shop
www.the-home-brew-shop.co.uk

Brewstore
www.brewstore.co.uk

The Malt Miller
www.themaltmiller.co.uk
Supplies many specialist beer ingredients.

The Somerset Distillery
www.ciderbrandy.co.uk
For apple eau de vie.

Black Cow
www.blackcow.co.uk
For a high class vodka made from milk.

Manufacturers

Ritchies
www.ritchieproducts.co.uk

Young's
www.youngshomebrew.co.uk.

Vigo
www.vigopresses.co.uk
Supplier of equipment such as presses and crushers for the cider maker.

Wyeast
www.wyeastlab.com
US manufacturer of yeasts (available in the UK) with an informative website.

Useful organisations

The Craft Brewers Association
www.craftbrewing.org.uk
A useful source of information about suppliers, and much more.

Dead Brewers Society
www.deadbrewerssociety.co.uk
For ancient beer recipes.

Books

The Oxford Companion to Beer
by Garrett Oliver
A very comprehensive guide to beer terminology and history.

Making Sparkling Wines
by John Restall and Donald Hebbs
Taking a more serious approach to sparkling wines.

Real Cider Making on a Small Scale
by Michael Pooley and John Lomax
Excellent advice and information for the home cider maker.

Acknowledgements

Few books are written without the assistance of others and this one is most certainly no exception, not even a bit. Chief among them are several notables from the world of brewing. They are, in no particular order: Coreen Barnett of Dorset Homebrew who has been tireless in answering my endless questions; the remarkable, generous and endlessly garrulous Alastair Wallace who knows more about beer than anyone I have ever met; Mark Jenkin of the Mighty Hop Brewery in Dorset who supplied several of the beer recipes and tolerated my questioning with grace; and Julian Temperley of Somerset Cider Brandy, Nigel Stewart of Bridge Farm Cider and the gentle Oliver Strong of Dorset Nectar who advised me on the fine art of cider-making. My sincerest thanks go to them all.

A few whose work does not involve brewing have been a help and an inspiration. Among them are Monica Wilde of Napiers Herbalists, Susanne Masters, collector and student of ethnic recipes and Dr John Cockrill, who has been kind enough to check my work to ensure I will not poison anyone, not too much anyway.

I would like to thank the companies Ritchies and Vigo for their advice and support. I am also most grateful to The Dead Brewers Society, which has been so gracious in allowing the reproduction of versions of their carefully conserved ancient beer recipes.

I have tested the patience of my friends from Bloomsbury more than usual but they have been as supportive, professional and charming as ever, so my thanks go to Xa Shaw Stewart, Natalie Hunt, Richard Atkinson, Marina Asenjo and Alison Glossop. I am also grateful to my project editor, the ever-subtle Janet Illsley, and to designer and beer enthusiast Will Webb.

Gordon Wise of Curtis Brown has been my steadfast guide, so thank you, Gordon. Thanks, also, to Antony Topping of Greene and Heaton, cheers to Rob Love of River Cottage who I hope will not be disappointed and finally, as always, thank you, Hugh, for your introduction and for entrusting me with yet another book.

Index

Page numbers in *italic* refer to the illustrations

River Cottage Handbooks

Mushrooms
by John Wright
introduced by Hugh Fearnley-Whittingstall

River Cottage Handbook No.1

Preserves
by Pam Corbin
introduced by Hugh Fearnley-Whittingstall

River Cottage Handbook No.2

Bread
by Daniel Stevens
introduced by Hugh Fearnley-Whittingstall

River Cottage Handbook No.3

Veg Patch
by Mark Diacono
introduced by Hugh Fearnley-Whittingstall

River Cottage Handbook No.4

Edible Seashore
by John Wright
introduced by Hugh Fearnley-Whittingstall

River Cottage Handbook No.5

Sea Fishing
by Nick Fisher
introduced by Hugh Fearnley-Whittingstall

River Cottage Handbook No.6

Hedgerow
by John Wright
introduced by Hugh Fearnley-Whittingstall

River Cottage Handbook No.7

Cakes
by Pam Corbin
introduced by Hugh Fearnley-Whittingstall

River Cottage Handbook No.8

Fruit
by Mark Diacono
introduced by Hugh Fearnley-Whittingstall

River Cottage Handbook No.9

Herbs
by Nikki Duffy
introduced by Hugh Fearnley-Whittingstall

River Cottage Handbook No.10

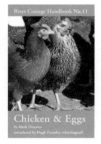

Chicken & Eggs
by Mark Diacono
introduced by Hugh Fearnley-whittingstall

River Cottage Handbook No.11

Booze
by John Wright
introduced by Hugh Fearnley-Whittingstall

River Cottage Handbook No.12

Seasonal, Local, Organic, Wild

FOR FURTHER INFORMATION AND
TO ORDER ONLINE, VISIT
RIVERCOTTAGE.NET